YOU GOTTA BE NUTS

TO OWN AN RV:

Reflections of a First-Time RV

Owner on a Trip to Alaska

Robert W. Pearson

DEDICATION

To my grandchildren: Lianni, CC, Benjamin, Mary Beth, Anna, and Jack. May your journeys through life be long, joyful, and interesting, with or without an RV

CONTENTS

1 PREFACE

Before you retire you think to yourself or confide in your wife, "Wouldn't it be great to own an RV and travel the country?" You picture yourself riding high and proud above people in little vehicles that can't carry a kitchen and toilet on their back, sleep seven, and store a six-pack of chilled Bud Light in a refrigerator just five steps behind your faux leather, swivel, captain's chair. There you are (in your mind's eye) powering down a highway in a vehicle that has the same aerodynamic qualities of a saltine cracker box on wheels. Like so many retirees, you think that traveling the country in a motorhome would be like an exotic expedition in Africa without the fear of contracting sleeping sickness from tsetse flies. You picture you and your spouse or partner winding your way across two-lane roads, off the beaten path, stopping to visit those small-town historic districts whose brown road signs beckon you to take the exit ramp off the interstate highway on which you now hurry to more important destinations. (Little do you know until you've fulfilled your dream of owning an RV that many of these historic districts are composed of one antique emporium, two poorly cleaned bars, and more than three boarded-up stores, the victims of the Walmart that supplies the locals with what the shops in town used to offer. But I'm jumping ahead. It's hard not to.)

There's much you don't know about owning and driving an RV if you've not already owned one. That's why I've written this book. I'm here to help you. I had long coveted owning an RV and took the leap with my wife, Wilma. Like many large purchases in our lives, we didn't do as much research as we should have. But we didn't have this book to consult either.

You might think from the tone and title of the book that I'm a complainer, a negative sort of guy who sees the glass half empty, who sees only the worst in people or events. That's not so. I'm a sweet fellow, voted "Most Popular" in my high school senior class more than 50 years ago. And to show you this, I've included in this book a chapter on "Travel Tips" and other sections where I note the good that can be found in the irritating, pestering, uncomfortable, and costly aspects of RVing. I also provide reflections on driving the coach we bought and the trip we took to Alaska, America's last wilderness, as they say, in the land of the midnight sun, as they also say.

* * *

Wilma and I had thought about buying an RV for several years, but our first serious step in that direction began with a course on RVing that was offered at a life-long learning program in Celebration, Florida where we had moved from New Jersey to flee cold, windy, grey winters in search of warm, sunny weather. The class filled an hour and a quarter each afternoon for three consecutive weeks. Our instructors had been RVing for about 40 years, spending long stretches of time without a house firmly anchored beneath their feet. They were kindly folks, both to each other and to the 25 students who peppered them with questions during each session. They're the type of people you'd want as an aunt and uncle growing up: caring listeners who want the best for you, knowing they don't have the obligation to pay your college tuition.

Most of the students in that class were like us: retired and looking to learn whether RVing was a silly fantasy or a realistic objective. There is an allure to RVing that we've witnessed in many retirees who don't have one. It's the freedom to go where you want, when you want, to be able to sleep in your own bed, to cook your own meals while traveling, and to bring your cat, dog, children, or grandchildren with you. (I'm convinced that many retired people buy RVs so that they can enjoy the companionship of their pets rather than their spouses.)

Most of the ideas that you find in this book arose from the silent monologues I had with myself while driving the RV. While these thoughts helped occupy me while making a thousand small adjustments to the steering wheel and distracted me from my worries that we'd be blown off the road, it was a challenge to remember them when I took my turn in the passenger seat to write them down. I was likely to forget the thought if it came early at my turn at the wheel. But a lost idea was no big deal in the end. I forgot I had the ideas I didn't remember.

2 Buying an RV

We pulled into the Florida State Fairgrounds on a sunny day in January for what was billed as "The World's Largest RV Show." Our mission: to check out as many RVs as we could that day and write down all the features that we would want in a used RV we would buy later. My wife recorded our wish list in a small notebook. The Fairground was a typical state fairground with buildings filled with vendors, and outside stands peddling corndogs, cotton candy, and fried turkey legs. The fried alligator tail was probably unique to a fair in Florida. Although thousands of RVs from all the major manufacturers jammed the fairgrounds, we limited our research to Winnebago models. We were told they were made in America. We later learned they were made in Iowa, and you can't get any more American than that.

We thought we would buy a used Class C so we began our research by visiting this type of coach. A class C is built on a standard cargo van base like a Ford Econoline. They're typically shorter and smaller than a Class A coach, which is the big, boxy vehicle that looks like a bus and that you see on highways sporting decals of swirls and swooshes running the length of the coach. Class C's typically have a bed above the driver and passenger area (called a "cab over") but can run more than 30 feet in length.

Class A's can be propelled by a diesel engine in the rear (which RVers called "pushers") or a gasoline engine in the front. They provide storage in the coach's underbelly or "basement" and panoramic views through large front windows that are expensive to replace when cracked by flying rocks in the Yukon and Alaska.

Class B's are the smallest class of RV. You'd think they'd fall between A & C in size, but why be so logical? They are distinguished from the Class C's by the absence of the "cab over" feature, but they too use a cargo van for their chassis. Everything about them is smaller, which means less storage and living space but better maneuverability, easier parking, and more miles per gallon of gasoline.

Fifth-wheelers are towed by another vehicle, typically a pick-up truck. No need to tow a car to visit destinations where RVs are unwelcome. Your pick up serves that purpose.

Our list of desirable features began to build as we inspected various models. The list grew to include adequate kitchen counter space for preparing meals; a bathroom with a shower big enough to bend over and turn around easily; a double sink to wash and rinse dirty dishes; a bed that could be accessed from three sides so that neither of us would have to crawl over the other in order to visit the bathroom during the night; a living space large enough to comfortably seat six for drinks and conversation; extra beds if the grandkids would ever join us on a trip; and automatic leveling jacks. We carried our list from display coach to display coach, but none of the models we visited checked all the boxes. One salesman we bumped into on the fairgrounds suggested we were looking for fools' gold when we told him of our mission that day. "You won't find an RV that has everything you want," he said. "But if you do, buy it on the spot."

We were ready to leave the show when we passed a Class A whose special show price was less than the more expensive Class C's we had just visited, so we entered the coach and began checking off one item after another on our list until Wilma declared aloud, "Oh, my God. This RV has everything we want." A salesman was standing nearby and heard Wilma's declaration.

"Are there any questions I can answer for you?" he asked, leaning over our shoulders. We asked a few, which he answered. When it appeared that our questions had run dry, he looked Wilma in the eyes and said, "Is there any reason you can't buy this coach today?"

"Nope," my wife said as her opening negotiation volley. *Oh my God*, I thought. *This guy's got our goose.*

Our intention to buy a used RV died on the spot and with it the advantages we would later better understand. Foremost among these are the many kinks that the manufacturer manages to build into a new coach, which the previous owner of a used RV straightens out. Obviously, used RVs cost a lot less than new ones, which was the original insight that drove our plan to buy one and that had just become a large -- and largely forgotten -- fact.

The disadvantages of a used RV are equally obvious. There's the wear and tear on the engine, drive train, tires, chassis, and other systems, stains on the carpets and dimpled foam cushions the shape of someone else's butt. Although you try to suppress the thought, you know that someone other than you or your wife farted on the driver and passenger seats. Probably a lot.

We agreed to take delivery from the dealership about a month after we signed the purchase papers at the show, thus following one of the cardinal rules of RVing:

Don't be in a hurry. The time would allow the dealer the opportunity to ensure everything was working by the time we picked it up. They offered – and we gladly accepted – the chance to camp in the RV at their site for one or more days to learn how it worked, to take a class on driving RVs, and to receive a walk-through of our coach from one of their mechanics.

We were surprised to learn when we went to take possession of the RV that the service representative assigned to us had no knowledge of the tow dolly that we had negotiated to receive at no additional cost when we purchased the coach at the show. (Apparently, we hadn't done as badly in the negotiations as I had feared.) We wanted to tow our Prius, what RVers call a "toad."

"Oh, you bought this from a 'show dog'," the rep told us. "We bring guys in from all over the country to help us sell models at large shows like Tampa." He said this in a way that led us to believe he was explaining why he had no knowledge of the deal we had struck but, more worrisome, to indicate they would not honor that agreement. Our voices grew louder, our hearts beat faster, and pained expressions ran across our faces as we threatened to walk away, not knowing whether that was possible. A series of conversations ensued between the rep and management beyond our ears and eyes. They relented. We had a tow dolly (albeit a used one).

We discovered several small defects in the coach's assembly, but one large one: The refrigerator didn't work when powered by electricity. RV refrigerators are sophisticated (and thus finicky) machines because they cool either by electricity or by propane gas, fed by – in our case – an 18-gallon tank that ominously rides in a compartment not far beneath the floor of the driver's seat. We would meet several RV owners during our trips that had similar problems with their refrigerators.

We reported the problem, leaving the RV at the dealership, and returned home in our car, an hour away, after being assured that the service engineers would run tests to identify the source of the problem and fix it. They did the former, but not the latter. They ordered a new refrigerator from Iowa and, after another two weeks, installed it. We were finally ready to roll.

3 OUR MAIDEN VOYAGE

We had signed up at the RV show to attend the Florida State WIT (Winnebago International Travelers) rally in Sarasota, Florida, which was not too far away in time or distance. It was the first of several "practice runs" we hoped to take in preparation for our planned journey to Alaska and back. We accepted final delivery of the RV on our way to the rally. I took on the task of driving the two hours and was terrified to learn how the RV stumbled down the road, knocked from side to side by gusts of wind and passing semis. It felt like a friend who puts his arms across your shoulder as he bumps his hip into yours, causing you to wobble as his hand holds you from falling to the ground. Stronger gusts of wind are more like being hit by a bumper car that rams into you at full speed from the side.

We nonetheless made it to the Florida WIT Rally. The volunteers at the welcoming table handed us a packet of information and advertisements, along with our name tags. At the bottom of the tags were green flags on which had been embossed in gold letters the words "First Timer." We came to discover that this designation served the same purpose as the sign "kick me" that someone taped to your back when you were a teenager walking down the hall in high school. We weren't physically accosted by veteran RVers, but the flag on our name tags encouraged all we met to share their most harrowing RV experiences.

A single catastrophe is more easily remembered than a hundred beautiful sunsets. And it's natural to tell well-rehearsed horror stories to someone you've just met because your wife has grown tired of hearing you recount them, no matter how much pleasure you take from describing the events leading to your death-defying experiences. These stories become part of the rite of passage for the novice RVer.

The stories of broken windshields, blowouts, and near-death experiences we heard at the rally scared us. (The thought popped into our minds that people who must have died while driving their RVs – surely there were plenty given the near-miss stories we were being told -- weren't there to tell us about their misfortunes.) We left the rally looking at each other with the same thought: *Did we do the right thing in buying our RV or did we make a huge mistake?* We'd spend the next year and 25,000 miles finding out the answer to that question.

4 THE BEGINNING OF OUR TRIP TO ALASKA

While waiting for paperwork to be processed on the purchase of our new RV at the Tampa show, we circled back to a booth at the fairgrounds that promoted membership in the Winnebago International Travelers (WIT) club. We consummated that membership by completing a form and swiping our credit cards. We also put our names on the waiting list for one of the two "Winnie" caravan trips to Alaska that were scheduled for later that summer. Our life-long learning teachers were team leaders of the caravan we would wait to learn if we would be allowed to join.

Caravans are groups of about 20 RVs that take a trip like the one to Alaska. The entire trip is planned for you and includes some group meals, tickets to events, and entry to attractions. The organizers provide a lead

RV that scouts for troubles on the road ahead and phones back such information to the RVs that follow. RVs in most caravans leave each camp site in small groups so not to form a train of RVs that other motorists are unable to pass. The group also includes a "tail gunner" who trails behind everyone and stops to help any RV in the caravan that experiences trouble. You can see the obvious advantages that such a trip provides, especially for nervous RV virgins like us.

We were seventh on the waiting list, a position that the organizers cheerfully assured us provided a not entirely remote chance of making it on to the trip. Subscriptions for caravans begin about a year in advance of the trip and we were told that many people withdraw from the trip as the date for departure nears.

We were also told by people at the Sarasota WIT rally that caravans on which they'd travelled were often "hurried." In other words, caravan planners scheduled frequent, but brief, stays at campgrounds along the way. You rarely stayed at any one location for any length of time while on the trail. The choice of how long to stay at any spot is not yours. And the odds were more than zero that tensions would likely arise after weeks on the road with any group of 40 or so strangers who come to learn you're an unpatriotic, dangerous, political idiot. These observations gave us pause. We tend not to join groups that would have us as members.

Alas, our position on the wait list didn't improve and Wilma began emailing and phoning campsites that roughly followed the trail of the Alaskan caravan, although at a slightly more leisurely pace. The trip we (more accurately -- she) planned would take about three-and-a-half months and nearly 14,000 miles. Wiser men and women might have hesitated to take on such an undertaking, but undertakers would not deter us.

* * *

I had originally thought to begin the journey part of this memoir/travelogue/advice book when we left Arlington, Virginia rather than our home in Celebration, Florida. Our stop in Arlington was a long-planned prelude to our journey to babysit granddaughters. We had made the trip to and from Arlington several times to visit the grandkids and their parents (otherwise known as our children) before we bought the RV, and I thought this leg of our trip would be uneventful. That was before I mangled the front left side of the front bumper on the Prius when backing it off the tow dolly and before we spent more than an hour trying to correct the tire pressure on the coach on the first morning of our journey toward Arlington.

I won't dwell on the bumper. We got it back on well enough to begin the trip. (See the tip about anger management in a subsequent chapter. It came in handy here.)

The tire pressure issue was more irritating. At the urging of someone we met on our maiden voyage at the Florida WIT rally, we purchased a tire minder. (We purchased several items that fellow RVers prompted us to do during the rally, the most valuable of which were stabilizing bars and heavy-duty shock absorbers that reduced the effects of crosswinds and passing semis by what seemed to be about 50 percent.) The tire minder consists of a controller that is a little smaller than a smartphone. It sits inside the coach and tells you from the comfort of the cabin the tire pressure from bottle-cap size devices that you screw onto every tire valve. The controller will alert you if the tire pressure falls above or below the recommended amount. It will flash a red light and beep if a tire's pressure departs from that level.

We purchased and had the device installed a week prior to our trip. The monitor certified that the tire pressure was good on all six tires of the RV when I turned it on for the first time. I turned it on again two days later at the storage facility where we kept the coach. The gauge on the right front tire read 58 PSI, far below the recommended 82. The gauge read 55 the following day when I returned.

We had purchased an extra tire for the coach in preparation for the trip to Alaska. Guidebooks, which my wife devoured, urged us to carry a spare. Surely, we weren't going to change any flat tire on a 30-foot RV. We had purchased insurance for towing and tire changing, but we were warned that Alaska and the Yukon don't grow 19.5-inch tires on hemlocks and, if we needed to replace one, could wait days for its delivery from the Lower 48. We both appreciated the irony of the situation. We bought a spare tire for the wilds of Alaska and now had to use it for the wilderness of Kissimmee, Florida.

We drove the coach, with spare, to a nearby Camping World (CW) where we had purchased the tire minder. Wilma told the CW service folks that the tires were OK before they installed the tire monitor because she wanted to implicate them in hopes of some compensation, prompt service or, perhaps, sympathy. The CW service guys said they would check it out. We left the spare with them.

I had tried to pump up the failing tire before driving to CW, but I couldn't get the wheel cover off the tire, which is required to place the electric air pump (one of the many additional purchases we made beyond the sticker price of the coach itself) onto the tire valves. The lug wrench that the manufacturer provides is useless. I would later buy a truck lug wrench to remove the chrome wheel covers but didn't have one at this point in our journey. N.B.: You need only (can only) remove two of the lug nuts on each wheel cover on the type of RV we have. These special nuts have dimples on them; the others don't. Do not try to remove the ones without dimples unless you want a hernia. They're permanently affixed to the wheel covers. (Now that I think of it, I may have tried to use the tiny lug wrench provided by the manufacturer to remove these permanent nuts, which could explain why the manufacturer's wrench didn't work and why I bent the tiny handle on that tiny wrench.)

While CW worked on the tires, we drove to the tire store from which we had purchased the RV spare to order a second and third tire, one for the Prius and another for the tow dolly. We were not taking any chances in Alaska and the Yukon. We'd stow the spares in the "trunk" of the Prius during the trip. We returned to CW to receive good news: the tire monitor wasn't installed properly, which caused a false reading. Everything was OK now. Tire pressure was 81 PSI and steady. Close enough.

Now back to the morning of Day 1 of our trip. We were in the coach at the storage facility. I turned the engine on, inserted the tire minder power converter into the cigarette lighter hole (otherwise known to younger readers as the 12-volt DC outlet). The red light came on and began beeping. Tire No. 5 (left rear inner tire on the RV) registered only 40 PSI. I got out of the coach to visually inspect the tire, which looked OK. But 40? Would we take the chance? No.

I retrieved the electric pump that runs off the 120-volt AC outlet (aka "the cigarette lighter hole"). Brilliant design. But the cord from the outlet to the pump was too short to reach the rear tires. It was useful only with front tires, a not so brilliant design after all.

I had a 50-foot extension cord that would easily reach the rear tires from one of the interior electrical outlets. I was beginning to think I was the one who's brilliant. I hooked it up and asked Wilma to crank the engine. The pump didn't whimper. I returned to the cabin and reset the GFCI outlet into which I had plugged the pump. Nothing again. I plugged the pump into the cigarette lighter outlet inside the coach to see if the pump was broken, and the pump's controls came to life. Unfortunately, the cord hadn't grown any longer with direct current coursing through its slender black vein. It was alive, but still useless.

"I wonder if these electrical outlets are working," I said to Wilma.

"They work. I've used them before," she responded.

Still trying to identify why the pump wasn't working, I went outside the coach to fetch an iron from one of the outside storage compartments. (Yes, the type of iron you iron clothes with. No, we're not that fashion-conscious. Wilma needed it to press the fabric she was going to use in sewing a quilt during the trip. No idle hands here. And yes, she also brought a sewing machine along with us.) I plugged the iron into an outlet to see if electricity flowed through the outlet by checking the iron's digital display. Nothing. The display did not come alive.

"The iron's not turning on," I said.

"Of course," Wilma responded. "The electrical outlets in the coach don't work unless the main is plugged into an external power source. The RV doesn't want you to use electrical appliances while traveling down the road."

Didn't she tell me five minutes ago that the outlets work? I thought to myself. (I carry on quite a few silent, solitary conversations.)

"Okay, let's drive back home. I'll use the front porch outlet and extension to pump up the tire." Remember, this is all happening on the first day of our trip. We had yet to leave town an hour after we had begun.

At home, extension cord plugged into the porch outlet, pump plugged into the extension cord, and control panel lit, which indicated the pump was now ready to go to work, I set the PSI dial to 82, attached the pump to the tire, and turned the pump on. Nothing, the operative word for the morning. The gauge on the pump told me that the tire was already at 83 PSI, not 40! The tire pressure was fine. The tire minder wasn't. *I'll be a sweaty s.o.b.*, the internal conversation continued. "Let's get going," I said aloud.

* * *

We pulled in front of daughter and son-in-law's house on Monday afternoon. The coach would stay there for the next eight days when we would begin our journey to Alaska with serious intent. Although we had to fetch clothes and stuff from the RV from time to time (we would be spending nights in the house), we thought the coach wouldn't bother us for a while. Wrong. After two days, the steps wouldn't retract. We tried to contact people who would come on site to fix it but didn't receive any response within the first day of calls (we would eventually). Wilma fired up YouTube and discovered we were not the first RVers with unretractable steps. The videos displayed a variety of potential problems. We surmised from viewing a half dozen or so DIYer-fixer-uppers that ours was an electrical problem.

The following morning, I crawled under the coach and found an electrical connection to the steps. Before unplugging and re-plugging it, as one YouTube video suggested, I thought that, if successful, the stairs might retract into my skull. I crawled back from beneath the coach and opened its door so that the stairs wouldn't retract (they don't if the door is open), should I fix them with the unplug/replug technique. Death averted!

I crawled under the coach again, laying both a towel and yoga mat across the hard, grey street pavement. I slithered to the far side of the coach, rolled onto my back, grabbed the electrical plug, and pulled it apart. I adeptly re-plugged it, using my adverbial powers. The light under the stairs lit. *Holy cow, I did it.* I crawled out from under the coach and walked around it to the door, which I shut. The stairs retracted.

The next day, a strong storm passed across Northern Virginia on its way to the Jersey Shore. It left us a present: a large branch on top of our RV that was five inches in diameter at the point it had broken away from the hulking tree leaning over the RV. I would guess the total weight of the branch was about 120 pounds. Fortunately, the kid's house had both a ladder and saw for me to surgically remove the limb from the top of the RV, one branch at a time. And better still, there was no damage to the RV as far as I could tell. But now I had to add a saw to the tools we'd carry with us to Alaska, just in case.

And what about that tire minder? I succeeded in placing the caps on the car and tow dolly but couldn't get them to work on the four rear tires of the coach, which I had to reconfigure when adding two to the rear tires of the Prius and two from the tow dolly. I learned from talking with the manufacture's technical support that the air release pin inside the tire valve had to be far enough out to release a small puff of air when you screwed on the tire monitor caps. The tech support person told me I could adjust that pin with the tool that came with my kit, but no such tool came with the kit. I drove the car to an auto supply store to buy one, returned to the coach, fiddled with the air release pins on the RV's back tires, but still couldn't get the tire monitor to work on the RV rear tires. I gave up trying.

We left Tuesday afternoon on our quest to Alaska, or as one of the granddaughters would say, "Africa." Wilma, planner-in-chief, had chartered a short four-hour trip for the day, and two hours into the trip, phoned ahead to reserve a pull-through campsite at a campground near Somerset, Pennsylvania. (She had made reservations at most of the campgrounds we would stay during the trip. This campground was one of the few she did not.) The campground was about eight miles outside of town, off a two-lane highway that rose and fell across dark green hills dotted with widely scattered barns and farmhouses. The campground sat comfortably amid those rolling hills. Although the camp's brochure declared that it was established in 2004, the office, bathhouse, and hookups all appeared to be a more recent vintage. Clean and quiet, the place called us to stay longer, but we had to move on to Cleveland the next day to visit our son and his fiancé.

We both had a restless night's sleep. I was awoken by the cold that rushed through all the windows that we had foolishly left open that night. And Wilma and I were also both aroused by the night's silence. Yes, hearing nothing can awaken you. The wail of a train's horn would awaken us often on the remainder of our journey's way.

One good thing about operating a motorhome is the appreciation you develop for the government's role in infrastructure development. We couldn't have traveled like we did without the roads and bridges that we crossed, which were not available to the prospectors and stampeders for gold during the Yukon and Alaska gold rushes of the late 19th and early 20th centuries. You also grow to appreciate another element of public infrastructure: public sewers. Waste management is part of your job on an RV. It's a visible reminder that waste is a part of life, especially if you've got clear plastic sewer elbows. It's not something you flush and forget about on an RV, which requires you to eliminate the eliminated from time to time.

5 On Driving

I thought and wrote during our trip to Alaska about life in St. Louis as a kid. I was writing a memoir about growing up there, which my upcoming high school's 50th reunion inspired me to pen, and long hours in the driver and passenger seats afforded the time to do. We planned to attend the reunion in late September on our way back to Florida as the denouement of our trip to Alaska for me. (Wilma's would be the National Quilt Museum in Paducah, Kentucky a few days later.) I also thought while driving or sitting in the passenger seat about our experiences in the RV. Much of the book you're now reading was drafted while riding in the passenger seat.

We've each now driven our RV more than 10,000 miles. But my blood pressure still rises – although much less than when I started driving our RV – when an 18-wheeler passes and a trailer wall of about 10 by 40 feet rolls past the left side of my face. The vantage afforded by sitting as high off the ground as you do in a Class A is more unsettling to me than the view from a car. There, you see wheels and the undercarriage of the truck with open space beneath it, which is less threatening than the wall that moves by you at what feels to be a foot away.

Beware of cars for they know not what they do

Wilma and I slow down to allow cars merging from an entry ramp onto the highway. It doesn't always work out well. Some car drivers don't realize that their car is so much more agile and able to accelerate than our lumbering cracker box. Maybe they slow down because we're so big, but whatever the reason, the game of who can go the slowest frustrates us. Most car drivers also don't know that it takes an RV about twice the distance to stop as it does their car. We keep a safe distance between us and the car or truck ahead in recognition of this fact, not because we want cars to dart between us or turn into our lane with a mere foot to spare between their back bumper and our front.

There is a corollary to this caution about car drivers: new RV owners aren't necessarily good RV drivers and since you don't know who's the novice and who's the experienced RV driver, stay clear of all of them if you're driving a car. Indeed, it's somewhat frightening to learn that RV drivers are not required to be trained or licensed in driving an 18,000 pound vehicle. I suspect that many fewer RVs would be sold if that was required and if you got to test drive one before you decided to purchase it.

Replacement parts while on the journey

I visited Ford dealerships throughout much of British Columbia, Canada on our way to Alaska. It's not that I have a fetish for them. I was looking for two parts for our RV: an oil filling cap and a windshield washer hose bulkhead fitting for a Ford V-10, our coach's chassis. The cap fits over the tube into which you pour motor oil. The RV shop at which I had the oil changed before embarking on our trip to Alaska apparently forgot to put the cap back on, which I didn't discover until I opened the "hood" in a campground outside of Glacier National Park in Montana (guess I should have checked under the hood sooner). The windshield washer hose bulkhead fitting (whose name I learned by looking at photos on the Internet) connects a tube from the windshield washer reservoir to another tube that feeds the soap onto the window from the wiper. The dealerships I visited stocked neither part, but I did enjoy asking for them, especially the fitting. I practiced saying "windshield washer hose bulkhead fitting" before I entered each showroom, which I would then scan for the sign that declared "Parts" sold here, even when the ones I needed weren't.

I would articulate those five words clearly and slowly. I couldn't help but think that the part's guy was impressed as he searched his computer screen for the location of that part among the shelves behind him. "What year is your RV?" he'd ask, pecking away at his keyboard. Another minute would pass. More keys stroked. He'd then look up from his terminal and say to me, "Sorry, you'll have to go to the source for that one." *I guess he means Amazon.com*, I thought to myself.

I hate driving the RV across tall bridges

I hate driving the RV on tall bridges, especially those that span bodies of water. I'm less fearful if the bridge crosses over terra firma. It's as if I wouldn't mind a gust of wind blowing the RV off the bridge if it landed on solid ground. A crushed chest or broken neck is preferable to drowning. I get a funny feeling down below when I drive across a tall bridge. My colon wants to hide beneath a blanket in a dark corner.

My wife's driving

My wife and I shared driving on all our trips, the short weekend practices as well as the journey to Alaska and back. We each took about two-hour turns at the wheel. This may not seem noteworthy except that it's my impression from talking to other RVers that it's not common. "Your wife drives too?" was a question asked by men when the topic arose in conversations at campgrounds. "Oh, I'm not about to drive that thing," was a refrain from women I spoke to on our trips.

My wife's a good driver. She probably even thinks she's better than me. But that's an argument in which we don't engage. It can't be won by either of us, so what's the point if victory cannot be achieved? I argue for points, not for the sake of argument.

Now there are a couple of things that we agree upon. Both us know when the other is driving too fast, especially around curves. We begin to lean into the curve as if our body's weight will prevent the big rig from careening off the road, falling helplessly into a ravine below, leaving no evidence, no mark of our misfortune, never to be found, our bodies .... Never mind.

We also know when the other is driving too far to the right of the road. That's when we grab the arms of the passenger seat or cusp our hands over our eyes while in that imposed darkness we picture the coach careening off the road, never to be found by another passing vehicle.

Division of labor

A certain division of labor arises in operating an RV, much of which I guess carries over from the division of labor that evolves in one's household. My wife cooks at home. I do the dishes (well, the ones she leaves me to wash). In the RV, I hook up the water and plumbing; she connects the electricity and cable. (Okay, there's no analogy to that in the house.) I mop the floors. She makes the bed. She drinks club soda. I drink wine. She jogs an hour each day. I take naps.

The five percent rule

I divined the five percent rule while driving the RV, but it applies across a broad range of human behavior and attitudes. Stated briefly, the rule reads as follows: within any large group of people, you will find a minimum of five percent who act or think differently from everyone else, no matter how odd, different, or inconsiderate that behavior or thought is. In the context of driving the RV, the rule applies to cars being driven by people acting like jerks. These include drivers who cut in front of you, weave in and out of traffic, tailgate, drive 20 miles per hour faster than all other traffic, and blow horns at the slightest provocation. I observed these behaviors while driving our RV, but realized that not everyone drives this way, nor does everyone drive this way all the time. But there's some percentage you can be confident you'll observe during your turn at the wheel. It's at least five percent.

Note that these behaviors are specific to driving and would not, therefore, apply to, say, a crowd in a packed football stadium. There, the five percent rule would apply to the minimum percentage of fans who shout obscenities at opposing players within a few seats of families with small children and those who spill beer down the backs of people seated in front of them. Thus, we have the second general characteristic of this rule: it varies by circumstance, setting, time, or context. (The first general characteristic of the rule is that it applies only to large groups of people. Don't ask me how large. I'm still working on it.) It can change over time. You can be among the five percent who act like a scoundrel at a football game one week and not the next. Or you can behave poorly at the stadium but not on the road to and from it.

The third characteristic of the rule is that it defines a floor. There can be more than five percent, but you will find at least that percentage of the population who demonstrate such a characteristic. For example, five percent of people who voted for Hillary Clinton agreed to a survey question that she supported a child sex ring out of the back of a pizzeria in Washington, DC. Yep, five percent of those who voted *for* Hillary Clinton said that she supported the child sex trade. Now, these voters could have thought the question was ridiculous and answered that way because they were irritated that the question was asked in the first place. Or maybe they misunderstood it. But consider the fact that 14 percent of those who voted for Donald Trump agreed with that statement and some idiot made a crusade from North Carolina to the pizzeria where the alleged child sex ring was being run and fired an assault weapon to make sure everyone in the pizzeria knew he meant business. He was arrested.

I'll conclude my thesis about the five percent rule by providing three additional supporting facts. First, psychologist Jerome Kagan reports that about five percent of irritable infants cannot be soothed by their parents. Second, five percent of the adult American population watch both MSNBC and Fox News. And third, about five percent of Americans believe cigarette smoking and lung cancer are unrelated.

Speed limits are for RVs

We all know that posted highway speed limits understate the speed at which you can drive without being slapped with a speeding ticket. That speed is eight miles an hour faster than the one posted. This rule, however, does not apply to RVs. If you're driving an RV, you should drive no faster than the posted limit.

Why? It's a safe speed for wrestling your rig around a curve without feeling the top of it about to tip over. It's also a comfortable speed for snuggling into that right lane, allowing miscreants to pass you on your left. And driving on a two-lane highway with no shoulder poses a problem for pulling over if a police car signals you to do so for speeding. What are you supposed to do: keep driving until there's a place you can pull off the road without falling into a ditch? And what if that stretch of road doesn't come your way for about 20 miles? Can you imagine the ticket you'll get by ticking off a cop who follows you with lights flashing for that distance? (Of course, the same chilling question arises about pulling over if you get a flat tire on a two-lane highway with inadequate shoulders to shoulder your coach's girth and weight.)

The benefits of extra weight

Water and gas are heavy. Filling both tanks will make your vehicle heavier, thus reducing gas mileage and adding wear and tear. But **one good thing** about a heavier coach is its greater ability to withstand buffeting crosswinds and passing semis.

6 On RV Campgrounds

We've stayed at more than 60 campgrounds so far. Some are filled with wide, full service, drive-through parking spots, which make hook up and departure easy, especially if you're towing a car. Some have cable TV hookups, some don't. WiFi works well at some. Others require you to take your computer to the laundry room, next to the manager's office (even when they advertise on their websites that they have free Wi-Fi). Some restrooms are spotless, the owners friendly and helpful. Others? You get the point. Wilma studied RV campground books and websites for reviews of potential campgrounds, but these weren't always accurate and sometimes you had to take what was available at the distance you wanted to travel that day.

Many RV campgrounds are understandably located next to a major highway. Although the whir of cars and trucks traveling 75 miles an hour 100 yards from your

RV campsite may fade into white noise until about midnight when it nearly stops, the restart of that traffic at 4 a.m. is likely to break your sleep. Throw in the trains that blare their long, long, short, long warning at nearby crossings, and you've got a night filled with short spans of sleep and interrupted dreams.

Managing RV campgrounds

It must be hard to run an RV campground. You can see it in some of the managers' eyes and read it in the signs like those in a bathroom of a campground near Wasilla, Alaska: "It's not the responsibility of employees of this campground to flush or plunge your mess." It doesn't take a hundred campers to provoke such a response. It can only take one to ruin it for everyone who follows when he clogs a toilet with waste and half a roll of toilet paper and doesn't bother to use the plunger that sits next to the toilet. Instead, he leaves his mess for someone else (maybe me, maybe the manager) to remedy. Campers usually have the option of moving to the next stall. The manager doesn't. He must fix the problem the next day and swears to himself that he's sick and tired of lowlife RVers. He sits at his computer after making his rounds and prints his signs and tapes them to every stall in the bathhouse. He may realize as the printer spits out his admonishments that they won't change a jerk into a model citizen, but it makes him feel a little less angry for a while.

The five percent rule applies to unflushed toilets in RV campground bathhouses. You'll open the door to the toilet to be greeted by an unflushed toilet approximately five percent of the time. I don't fully understand the cause of this phenomenon but I have two hypotheses. First, automatic flush toilets have become so pervasive that people either forget or have forgotten how to flush. Second, many people have their deepest thoughts while sitting on the throne. It is rumored that Martin Luther, for example, divined his 95 Theses that he would nail to the door of the Wittenberg Castle church in 1517 while taking a crap on his chamber pot. (Thomas Crapper would not invent his flush toilet until the late 1800s.) In other words, people may forget to flush, not because they no longer know how, but because they're trying to remember things before they can get back to their coach and write them down. Perhaps you too can launch something like the Protestant Reformation from a thrown at a KOA.

Showers

Plumbers in one campground installed the shower head when the average height of an adult male in the United States was 4 feet 6 inches, which was in the year. . . NEVER!

Many shower stalls in campgrounds throughout the United States measure about 2 ½ feet by 2 ½ feet. I'd forewarn you to be prepared to jump away from the cascading water when it changes from pleasantly hot to ice cold, but there's no place to jump except out of the shower stall altogether, and that's not always practical or possible.

I encountered one of the more bizarre showers in a private campground outside of Prince George, British Columbia. The changing area was large, about four by seven feet, with a black rubber floor mat that you see in bathhouse showers. They keep your feet off the concrete floor and guard against slips and falls. (No telling whether they harbor germs, fungus, mold or other sickening creatures.) This area also had a folding chair. Nothing unusual about these features except the size of this area, which was larger than most. Three hooks for clothes and towels hung from the left wall about three feet from the shower. There were no other hooks to hang a towel or the clean clothes that waited for you when you finished showering. A shelf for soap and shampoo hung outside the shower stall to the left of the curtain. Below it hung the faucet, also outside. The shower itself – prefab plastic – was about two by two foot in width and depth. You turned the shower on outside the stall, sticking your hand inside the curtain to test the temperature. You entered the shower into the streaming water but had to exit it to turn the water off, water from your body falling to the rubber mats.

Seasonal campers

Most RV campgrounds include spots for RVs that move from the lot of the dealer to a spot from which they rarely, if ever, move again. These are called seasonal RVs and are typically fifth wheelers. Their "season" will depend on the part of the country where the campground is located. In South Jersey, for example, the season would run from late Spring to early Fall, after which owners would drain the plumbing system and shut down the coach until they return to reawaken it the following Spring.

Most of these sites are as much "weekenders" as they are seasonal. Owners drive from Philly to the Jersey Shore, Manhattan to the Poconos, or Pittsburgh to the Laurel Highlands to take up residence for a couple days each week during the "season."

You can tell which RVs in a campground are seasonal. Many are vacant during weekdays. Many have patios or decks or permanent structures like screened porches. Some are elaborately landscaped. Some sit atop cinder blocks. Their owners brand their sites with a nameplate hung from a wrought iron stake or the coach's front door if a plastic flower wreath doesn't already hang there. Some have solar-powered lanterns that throw off enough light to identify only the location of the lamp itself, which I guess is ok if you know that there's nothing to trip on beyond its faint glow. All the ornamentation is there to tell any passerby that the people who live there (from time-to-time) are special, unique, one-of-a-kind, fun-loving personalities. Maybe they are.

7 What's Up with Dat?

- The South Dakota Visitors' Guide recommends you see the Lewis and Clark Visitors' Center. It's in Nebraska. What's up with dat?

- We had been traveling along I-90 just North of the Badlands in South Dakota for miles when I spotted an exit for 238th Street. Where were the other 237 streets we didn't pass? What's up with dat?

- Big city. Bad air. You buy an RV to get out into the country where the air is clean, crisp, and refreshing. Your campground may be near a highway and railroad track, but there's not a lot else around except for grass, trees, and other carbon absorbing flora. This is especially true in Big Sky country in the American West.

Yet you pull into a campground and, if the weather and temperature are right, you'll see scores of RVers sitting around campfires (not all campgrounds allow them). On especially calm nights – the safest night to light a campfire – the smoke hovers among the rigs, choking your view, fogging your head, and scratching your throat. Your view seems like you're looking through eyeglasses that haven't been cleaned for a month. When tired of the campfire, RVers re-enter their air-conditioned coaches to flee from the smoke. Maybe cities aren't so bad after all.

- I was struck as we crossed the Midwest of the number of large, one-story manufacturing buildings that we passed in remote, unpopulated areas. But the parking lots surrounding these buildings were populated by only a handful of cars, a sign that these were highly automated manufacturing sites, adding value to the national economy but few jobs.

- One of the worst stretches we drove across was just south of Beaver Creek in the Yukon. It was a 100-yard patch of loose gravel where the Territory was experimenting with different techniques for combatting the frost heaves that turned highways throughout the Yukon and parts of Alaska into roller coaster rides. I'd say the experiments were failing by the condition of that section of road. On the other hand, one of the official descriptions of these experiments cautioned that they weren't looking for only one solution to solve every challenge. They apparently have succeeded if you believe "not one" and "none" are the same.

- We stayed at two campsites during our journey that served an "all you can eat" pancake breakfast for a reasonable price. You'd begin with two pancakes. Coffee and sausage were extra. But in both cases, I could only eat the two pancakes and they sat in my belly like an overblown life preserver for the remainder of the day.

- My wife would torment me with the windshield wipers, not turning them on or off in what I would consider a "timely manner." Why doesn't the RV come with a twin set of windshield wiper controls with a switch that would allow me to control their use and speed (whether as driver or passenger)?

- Some of the small facts you discover along your way crush long-held beliefs. I, for example, had believed that "the rain in Spain falls mainly on the plain." But plains are grasslands for a reason. Trees require an amount of water that grassland climates do not provide. Grasses thrive where enough rain falls to prevent deserts from forming, but not enough for forests to flourish.

- Why do RV campgrounds design their sites such that your neighbor on your right hooks his sewer hose near your site's picnic table? These hookups are "closed" systems and we didn't smell refuge, but I still couldn't help thinking about the material that snaked its way through those tubes into a hole in the ground as I ate my burger. Only two of the sixty or more campsites where we camped had adjoining sites that coaches pulled into from opposite directions, thus putting the sewer connections near each other and on the side opposite the coach doors and picnic tables.

- Many of the towns in Alaska like Wasilla and Palmer seemed to have more churches than gas stations. Maybe more souls are running on empty than are cars.

- You visit a small town in a remote part of, say, South Dakota and discover that a music festival or local art show is scheduled there two days after your scheduled departure. You're crestfallen. "Oh shoot. I wish we could have gone to that," you say to your wife.

A week later you're in Dawson City, Yukon on the weekend of their annual music festival. "Damn. Look at all these people," you now say to her.

Restaurants and sidewalks are filled with disgusting, inconsiderate tourists. The towels to dry your hands are thrown across restroom floors. Motorcyclists shatter sound barriers. We couldn't get away from the festival fast enough.

- Museums, visitor centers, and education and cultural centers vie for the tourists' attention and money. They're often worth visiting. Some, like that at Haynes Junction in Alaska, are surprisingly sophisticated and well appointed. But we came across no museums and education centers to tell the stories of U.S. interstate highways, or the history of corporate welfare, or the decline of small-town America.

- We had stopped at the River's Edge campground in Fairbanks, Alaska. The weather was warm as it can be in mid-summer, and we had opened the windows of the coach to welcome a faint breeze inside. I was listening to "In a Parade" from Paul Simon's latest album. The song ended and before the next one began I thought I heard the nearby Yukon River flowing toward the Bering Sea, the relentless sound of life-granting, clean, turquoise water moving across beds of rocks deposited thousands of years ago by rivers of flowing ice, waters now bound by manicured lawns and tree-lined shores.

No. It was the sound of the air conditioning unit atop the RV next to ours.

- We saw pigeons in Alaska and seagulls in Montana. We saw hay being grown in the deserts of California and Arizona, hay that was fed to cattle who live in the shade of sheds that cover acres. We saw acres of freshly planted pistachio and almond trees that require large amounts of water to thrive in California's central valley along with hand-made signs complaining about irrigated water not being diverted from others' lands.

- The exterior of our RV is fiberglass. So too is the roof. The interior ceiling has a padding of foam an inch thick. None of this is sufficient to muffle the sound of rain and the drumbeat of hundreds of drops hitting your roof while you try to sleep.

- You buy an RV in part to take those scenic routes you've been too busy to travel before. You're now travelling off the beaten path along beautiful two-lane roads only to discover that you can't enjoy the scenery if you're driving. You're too busy keeping your eye on the road and the rig in the middle of your narrow lane, away from oncoming traffic on your left and the ditch on your right. There is no shoulder. There may as well be no scenic scenery.

- The first visitor's center you come across in Missouri along Highway 40 when entering from Oklahoma is 100 miles from the border. I guess the "Show Me State" wants to see a commitment on your part before it welcomes you. What's up with dat?

8 Radio Torture

We were traveling west on some road in the middle of America. I was reading Stephen King's memoir about writing. Wilma was driving. She started to fiddle with the RV's console. The radio went on. I looked up from my book. *Why in the world did she turn the radio on?* You couldn't hear what was being said above the roar of the tires, the rattle of the driver-side shade screen, the clank of plates and silverware with each crack and dip in the road. It could have been a sports channel – which she hates – for all you could tell from the noise. But a word or two surfaced above the din. I heard "administration," "President Trump," "Paul Ryan." My God. My wife had turned on a talk radio show. I hate them. At that moment I knew she was trying to torture me.

I put my book down. I couldn't concentrate. There was the chatter from the radio rising above the rattle of the rig. And there was the realization that Wilma was irritating me on purpose and succeeding.

She needed to stop after about ten minutes of this hell. A welcome center welcomed us. I pledged to myself to turn off the radio when I took over the reins of the rig. I volunteered to drive, although I hid my true motive for driving a half hour before my scheduled turn. We returned to the coach after a quick break. I took my place in the driver's seat and turned on the ignition. The talk radio show came on again. I hit a couple of buttons but failed to kill it.

"How do you turn off the radio?" I asked.

"I don't know. I don't even know how it turned on in the first place."

Damn.

9 Strip Poker in South Dakota

I stepped into the office/store at the Ponderosa Campground in White Sulphur Springs, South Dakota. The manager shouted from an adjoining room upon hearing me enter, "We're in here if you need any help?" I turned the corner toward the source of the voice and saw four people – two older, full-bodied women and two men of the same vintage -- playing cards at a long folding table.

"Is there gambling goin' on in here?" I asked.

"Sure is," a woman in a large one-size-fits-all red dress said. "Strip poker!"

"I guess you must have just started."

"Yep," she said. ""Cept I got my shoe off."

"You're on quite a losing streak," I responded and walked back to inspect the postcards, instant cappuccino mix, and handmade soaps among the hundreds of items neatly shelved, ready for purchase. After a minute, I overheard one of the men ask the woman in red, "What'd he mean: 'I guess you must have just started?'"

"We got all our clothes on, silly. That's why we 'musta just started.'"

I grinned and reached for a postcard depicting the White Sulphur Spring's City Hall facing a deserted main street.

* * *

One good thing about driving in a westerly direction in a rainstorm is that your destination for that day is likely to bathe in sun by the time you arrive. Because weather patterns tend to move from West to East, this good thing tends to work only when you're traveling westward. Another good thing about driving in the rain is that you don't have to clean dead bugs off your windshield when you stop for the night.

10 Allergies in an RV

My wife and I have a cat. Her name is Oreo because she is black with a white streak of hair running down her belly. She reminds you of an Oreo cookie when she lays flat on her side.

Unfortunately, I have an allergy to animal hair. I manage the allergy with Oreo well enough at home by taking a generic equivalent of Claritin, which is about half the price of that brand but has the same "active ingredient." I guess it's the inactive ingredients like marketing that produce the price difference. I get by at home on about one of these pills a week. If I catch the allergic reaction coming on soon enough, I block the red scratchy and tearful eyes, sneezing, and nasal congestion.

It's different in an RV. Start with size. It's a lot smaller than our house, which has many more distant corners for the cat's hair to congregate and many more places altogether that are beyond the reach of my nostrils. (Think about those balls of hair quarantined under the refrigerator or stove.) There are fewer places in the RV for Oreo to sleep (and she sleeps a lot) and these places (think bedspread next to my pillow) are returned to frequently to deposit nests of black hair. These problems are multiplied by rainy days when windows are closed and cat hair doesn't have the opportunity to be swept by the air into window screens.

I took to cleaning the coach about every other day to keep my intake of allergy pills to about the same frequency as at home. Although the drug manufacturers allege these pills to be non-drowsy, there must be other side effects to heavy intake of the drug. I noticed that my own hair seemed to have fallen out more rapidly while on our trip. Maybe I lost my hair in proportion to my reaction to another's.

11 Things Aren't Always What They Seem

We were heading down the Cassiar Highway in Canada. Wilma was driving and giving me a blow-by-blow description of our itinerary for the next five days when I saw, about 500 yards away, what I thought was a black bear walking down the highway. "Bear," I shouted, pointing, interrupting Wilma.

"If it's a bear," she said, "it's got brake lights."

Black bear sightings are common in Canada and Alaska. Indeed, park rangers are fond of telling visitors about what they call "bear rocks," which are nearly everywhere. Visitors to the parks on hikes will spot what they believe to be a bear sitting on the side of a distant hill contemplating its existence. You can tell the bear is deep in thought because it doesn't move no matter how long you stare at her, no matter how long the park visitor expects her to get on all four and walk away. She doesn't. She's a rock.

I guess a good part of our lives is spent figuring out what's real from what's not. There are no rules for doing so as far as I know. You just stumble along and hope your friends don't make too much fun of you along the way when you point to a bear rock.

* * *

One good thing happens to your house while you're away on a trip in your RV. It grows to twice the size you left it. At least that's what it feels like when you return home. Geez, there are different rooms you can visit. Seats at the kitchen countertop. What spacious luxury you'll enjoy when you return home.

A good thing also happens to your car after you've driven your RV for long distances. It becomes much more enjoyable to drive than it did before. It becomes quieter, smoother, more comfortable. Our Prius even became a sports car: agile and low to the ground, quicker to respond to a depressed gas pedal than our lumbering RV.

I didn't realize how windy North America is until I drove an RV. I also didn't realize how badly maintained roads, highways, streets, and bridges are. I had read about this decaying infrastructure problem but now I *know* about it: in my neck, my back, my butt.

12 Rusting Cars in Yards

Have you ever wondered why so many rural poor houses have so many rusting hulls of cars and pick-up trucks in their yards? I have. We saw them near Kitwanga, British Columbia and White Sulphur Springs, Montana. I think I've figured out why these artifacts are so prevalent in such areas, although I haven't confirmed my theory and may never do so. Here's my thesis in the form of a conversation in the house of a poor rural, Yukon family of five: Momma, Pappa, sons Bobby and Tommy, and baby sister, Sue Ellen.

Pappa, with partially chewed poutine in his mouth, turns to Momma and says, "Momma, I think it's time to retire old Betsy [a 1968 Ford pick-up]. She's got over 250,000 miles on her and I think she needs a new transmission and brake pads, and I bet somethin' else'll go haywire as soon as I fix those things. I think we can get by with the Chevy for a while until we save up enough for the down payment on another used truck."

Momma nods her head in agreement as she takes a bite of meatloaf she made for Sunday's supper.

"It ain't worth driving all the way into Smithers to sell her to that used car guy on Main Street," Pappa continues. "Hell, it'd cost us more in gas than that old swindler would be willing to give us for the pickup."

Pappa forks another cheese curd, along with a fry, and drags them across the brown gravy, losing a drop to his shirt as he raises it to his mouth.

"I've got some cinder blocks in the garage that I'll prop under the truck tomorrow. I'm gonna let the air out of the rear tires and take 'em off. They've only got 40,000 miles on 'em and I figure I can use 'em for another 20,000 on the Chevy when it needs 'em. I think the air filters are pretty new too and I'll get as many parts as I can off it. You never know when you might be able to use 'em."

Turning to his two sons, Pappa says, "Now I don't want you two boys using Betsy for target practice. Leave the damn truck alone. Ain't no good reason for you two to go shooting at it or kickin' in the fenders or throwing rocks at it. Just leave it alone, eh?"

Bobby looks at his dad and says, "No problem pops. Sure thing." He continues to look at his father until the old man dives his fork into another helping of poutine. Bobby looks toward his brother Tommy with a grin and a wink. They both know what they'll do to Betsy. The family continues eating. It's been decided and confirmed by the ensuing silence. Another pick-up truck will adorn the front yard, resting on the spot it last saw life.

13 Road Conditions

There are long stretches of interstate highway in the United States and Canada that are in bad shape. South Carolina seems to have its fair share on I-95 where concrete patches and gaping seams jar the coach every half second. Bop. Two bops per second. Bop. Bop… Bop. Bop… Bop. Bop… Bop. Bop… Bop. Bop… Bop. Bop. It's enough to drive you mad.

I thought about the sound the coach made crossing these concrete patches and seams in the road while driving. I tried to translate the sounds the tires made into a word. At first, it was a clop, but that was too sharp a sound. The actual sound was duller. Bop. That's it. Bop! Don't laugh. It kept my mind occupied for about 20 minutes. I had to rush to my pen and notebook at the rest area 25 miles later, lest I forget this aural discovery.

It helps to have a vivid imagination while driving an RV. What are you to do mile after mile on open highway but think about stuff? But you can only plan how you'll spend the $150 million you expect to win in the lottery so many times. You entertain yourself with other thoughts. You can't listen to a book on tape or to music. It's too darn noisy. The idea to write this book came to me while driving the RV. The story of my wife torturing me with the radio was the first thing I wrote.

Rock and roll and road signs

Nearly all the roads we traveled between Arlington, Virginia and Wyoming were broad, four-lane, divided highways. There was little to complain about. We traveled in northern Indiana, Illinois, Minnesota, and South Dakota across flat fertile fields of young corn and soybeans or tall grasses waving to cars and trucks passing along these rolling ribbons of concrete.

But there is a stretch of Interstate 80, South of Chicago, that has so many ripples on the pavement that it felt like you were sitting in a pulsating, coin-fed, almost-leather massage chair in a terminal at O'Hare airport.

The roads in Alaska and the Yukon can be far worse. Crossing from the Yukon into Alaska we entered a stretch of the Alaskan Highway that ran ahead of us like dips on the rails of a roller coaster. There were strips of loose-gravel road in the Yukon and Alaska that felt like you were driving over a two-lane washboard nearly a mile long. You were fortunate if there were no other vehicles in front of you so you didn't have to eat their dust.

* * *

Wilma was driving. "Slow down!" I said.

"I'm going slow," she said.

"Well then, go slower." The comfort level of a passenger must be 5 to 10 miles per hour slower than the one whose hands grip the wheel, a foot depressing the gas or brake pedal. As a passenger, I feel good about traveling 60 mph. As a driver, 65.

Observing (i.e., complying with) road signs will help you avoid some road mishaps, but not always. A rock thrown into your windshield by a fast-moving truck coming from the opposite direction is not uncommon and can't be avoided in the Yukon and Alaska. We had it happen to us. Four times. All 20 coaches of a caravan we met at Destruction Bay, Yukon Territory had at least one window damaged.

* * *

Highway 4 out of Valdez, Alaska was so bumpy that the fillings fell out of my teeth, my spinal cord compressed from repeatedly hitting the ceiling, and I lost 12 inches in height. It was so bumpy that I felt like a Bobble Head doll on steroids, and the eggs in the RV refrigerator scrambled inside their shells. Man, it was bumpy.

The highways that we drove in and around Los Angeles are as bad as those in the Yukon and Alaska. Obviously, their disrepair has different origins, but the roads are nonetheless equally bone-jarring. They were so bumpy in LA that our GPS began operating under the NFL's concussion protocol. The GPS was knocked so silly that it directed us to a highway that took us in the wrong direction. Wilma turned the wacky thing off and re-entered our destination. Only then did it come back to its senses and put us on the right path again.

Road repairs

The Yukon and Alaskan highway repair crews are busy through the summer months, matching long hours of sunlight with long working days. Makes sense. You can't repair roads when it's 40 degrees below. This, of course, poses a problem for the traveler. These repairs delay and frustrate the motorists and trash your car or coach as you travel over loose gravel and through clouds of dust, always fearful that a rock will crash into your windshield. Visit in early summer and you'll face roads that winter temperatures, ice, and snow abused. Wait a while and you'll face patches of unfinished repairs. It's like taking pills to offset the side effects of other medicines. Leave early and your back pain flares up. Leave late and you've got to take a laxative to loosen up the constipation that your painkillers induce. Your pick: back pain or constipation.

We crossed through many river gorges that had cut deeply into the earth, leaving canyons difficult for motorists to navigate. But they do along roads carved on the face of mountain walls. And to protect cars from falling into the canyons below, road workers have installed guard rails about two feet high. What? Two feet? How is that little rail going to stop a 12-foot tall RV from toppling over into the canyon? You know: never to be found by passing motorists.

Loose gravel

I asked a Canadian Mounted Policeman why loose gravel was used to repair roads in the Yukon Territory. He was sitting on a chair alongside an older man who had emigrated from Newfoundland to Carmacks, YT where Wilma and I stayed for a night on our journey northward. Carmacks is a small town with a well-stocked grocery store, motel, an adjoining RV campground, a modern-looking elementary school, and a few scattered houses on the Yukon River. It was there we saw a large black bear swim across the Yukon, climb up the embankment, and cross in front of our car on the road that ran parallel to the river.

"That's a good question," the Mountie said to my question about loose gravel. "I'm not quite sure. Probably costs less."

"Yep, that's probably it," the old timer said with a lilt common among Newfoundlanders who descended from Irish stock and who emigrated there in large numbers during the first two decades of the 20th century.

We knew well of the need to repair the roads. It seemed that the highways in the Yukon and Alaska move with the seasons. Frost heaves them skyward or fractures their surface in ways that create craters. Thaws will drop roads into mini-valleys with the rising temperatures of summer as the underlying permafrost withers under heated road surfaces. And it's not that these movements of pavement are even or symmetrical. The roads become more like rough seas that pitch the coach left and right as well as up and down. You can feel the top of the coach swaying, casting images in your mind of the RV tipping over on its side as you hold tightly to the wheel (if driving) and to the arms of the chair (if passenging).

The Canadian Highway Department must conspire with windshield makers. I now know why all the guidebooks and anyone with whom you talk about RVing to Alaska will talk about broken or cracked windshields. It's as popular a topic as fully extended RV awnings being sheered away by the wind. To their credit, the highway repair crews warn you about upcoming patches of loose gravel. Speed through them at your own peril, the peril of the car you're towing, and any trailing or oncoming vehicles.

During hot dry spells, these patches and longer strips of loose gravel will choke you in dust. You won't recognize your tow car after a day traveling through these obstacles. The toad will be covered with a film of dust and small rocks caked on the hood and front windshield. You hope that your next campground allows you to wash this paste off, but some RV campgrounds explicitly prohibit washing your coach or car at your site, although some provide coin-fed washing/rinsing wands at a station in the campground, which devour "loonies," Canadian coins with a loon on one side (N.B.: some of these carwash machines only accept old loonies that have a notch in them).

A mile is not a mile

Miles are longer in the Yukon than anywhere else we traveled. They're not literally longer. A mile is a mile. A kilometer, a kilometer (called "klicks" by young

Canadians). But they take longer to cross than elsewhere. Loose gravel, steep hills, and rough roads cause you to ease your foot off the gas pedal and lengthen your journey's time along each mile or kilometer you travel.

Other troubling aspects of travel in Alaska and the Yukon

There were a couple of unsettling aspects of traveling in Alaska and the Yukon, as well as Wyoming and Montana. One was the long stretches of road where you encountered no other vehicles. What if the RV broke down? How long would it take for rescue teams to find us?

The second unsettling aspect of traveling was the opposite of the first: watching large numbers of RVs returning to the Lower 48 states just as we were entering these areas. We crossed into Alaska toward the beginning of August because we had assumed that this month would be Alaska's warmest. It had been every place we had lived. I hadn't thought to look up the stats on this, which I did after our trip. It turns out that June and July are the warmest months in Alaska, not August.

Don't believe it

Never rely on a book older than a week to give you an accurate picture of the conditions of any stretch of the 1,500-mile AlCan highway or other roads in that part of North America. They change all the time.

And don't trust fellow travelers for their assessment of the roads. Their reports are as much a reflection of their personalities and dispositions as they are an accurate assessment of road conditions. "It's not as bad as they say," one fellow traveler told us about crossing "The Top of the World" passage in Alaska, not far from Dawson City. We declined to take this route nonetheless. Or: "The road is a total mess all the way from Whitehorse to Iskut" and "We hit a few dips in the road, but it was otherwise fine" are equally likely descriptions of the same piece of highway. One is offered by the proverbial optimist (who you may discover is a former truck driver) and the other is the assessment of someone who always sees the glass half empty.

* * *

The first gas sign you see in Canada will bring great joy. Get over it quickly. The sign tells you how many Canadian dollars it will cost you for a *liter* of gas, not a gallon. You know how many liters equal a gallon? Neither did I. It's about four! So, take that sign with the sweet looking number of, say, $1.10 per liter and multiply it by four to see that you'll be paying about the equivalent of $4.40 per gallon. (This was when the average price of a gallon of regular gas in the United States was about $2.20.)

14 On Language

We signed up for a boat tour of the Prince William Sound out of Valdez, Alaska in a small building surrounded by beautifully kept flower beds. After we bought the tickets, I asked the lady behind the counter if I could leave our car parked in her lot while we explored the town on foot. "Sure. But I close the fence at around 9:00 to keep the rabbits out. So, you have to be out by then." I didn't know what she meant but wasn't going to reveal my stupidity by asking. *Maybe 'rabbit' is an Alaskan word for some kind of unwanted tourist*, I thought.

We later discovered the source of her concern. There are wild rabbits hopping around Valdez who must love to chew on beautiful flowers.

Similar misunderstandings arose in asking for directions. "Excuse us," we began as we asked a tall grey-haired gentleman wearing cowboy boots, jeans, and a plaid shirt on a street in Valemount, British Columbia, "Can you tell us where the Post Office is?"

"Sure," he said. "Go down a block, make a left, and go two more blocks."

Simple enough. We followed his directions but found no post office. We later discovered that the "block" we were instructed to travel was a stretch of road about a mile long.

Or take the time we were in Prince George, BC when we were looking to buy a satellite phone because Verizon doesn't work in large areas of Canada, especially when forest fires destroy their communication towers. The store didn't sell them, but two salespeople suggested we go to *BK TwoWay* on 15th Street. One of the salespersons escorted us out the front door to give us directions. We understood him until he got to the part, "You can't miss it. It's right next to ICBC." Wilma and I looked at each other, grinned, and simultaneously asked, "What's ICBC?"

The salesman looked at us as if to say, *How can you not know what ICBC is?* But he didn't answer our question and returned to the store after we thanked him and headed back to the coach. We found *BK TwoWay*. They had no satellite phones to sell, although we did learn two things. First, satellite phones cost from $500 for the nearly useless to $1,600 for a good one. Second, the building next door to the store housed the Insurance Corporation of British Columbia, otherwise known as ICBC.

15 Road Signs

Construction/ Caution Loose Gravel/ Extremely Dusty
Conditions/ Be Prepared to Stop/ Max 70 km/h

These were the words printed on consecutive bright
reddish orange, diamond-shaped signs in Canada and
Alaska, spaced 50 yards apart. They grabbed your
attention and accelerated your heartbeat as you traveled
through road construction and repairs. They reminded
me of the rectangular, red signs of Burma-Shave that
my family looked for and read aloud in unison as we
drove two-lane highways from St. Louis to the Texas
Panhandle to see my grandparents on hot summer
vacations in the 1950s. The Burma-Shave signs

populated roadways until 1963. Their final slogan, spread across six signs, read:

Our fortune / Is your / Shaven face / It's our best / Advertising space / Burma-Shave

The Yukon and Alaskan highway departments should have copied Burma-Shave's ploy, spacing signs along the roadways under repair that might read:

Construction ahead/ Look for loose gravel/ And lots of dust too/ Duck when you see flying rocks/ And try not to feel blue/ Yukon [or Alaska] welcomes you

Are you kidding me?

We read the following road sign 10 miles west of Elk City, Oklahoma and again near Tulsa: "Hitchhikers may be escaped inmates" or another in Oklahoma: "Do not drive into smoke." "Leave your cell phone alone. Don't fall into bad habits," an electronic sign shouted outside of Tulsa, OK. Another in Homer, Alaska read "Do Not Pass Snow Plows on the Right."

Alaska and the Yukon are tough places to live and to drive. The road signs tell part of this story. "Avalanche Area," "Flying Debris," "Tsunami Evacuation Route." I was always relieved when we passed a sign informing us that we had successfully crossed the avalanche or slide zone without being crushed. And then there were wordless signs with three hills that meant you faced the possibility of tearing your back bumper off if you hit the approaching dips too fast.

I think one of the Yukon's biggest natural assets is rock. Glaciers messaged them into smooth orbs. Rivers and streams polished them. Machines pulverize them into gravel, which truckers carry from one point in the Territory to another to resurface highways that are convulsed by melting permafrost or cratered by potholes. This gravel becomes the projectiles that crack windshields and headlights on cars and RVs alike. Have I told you about cracked windshields?

16 The Lumber Mill

We pulled into an RV campground in Kitwanga, British Columbia, across the street from a lumber mill. The machinery of the mill was about a quarter mile from our parked coach, but we could see acres of timber across the road, waiting to be made into boards that you might buy at Lowes in Rio Grande, New Jersey. I had the idea to go to the mill to see if they would show me how logs were made into lumber. I felt like a kid, but what was there to lose?

I drove to the mill on Tuesday morning, while Wilma caught up with her business over a fickle Internet. I parked at a trailer that looked like offices and walked in. No one was there, but I could see that workers used the place to take a break or eat lunch. I stood outside for a while when a worker in bright but worn, fluorescent lime green vest, hard hat, protective glasses, and ear protectors walked briskly toward me from his workstation about 100 yards away. I walked toward him to close the distance between us. As he tilted one of his ear protectors away from his head, I told him I hoped to tour the mill. He pointed to a large building beyond the men stacking lumber and said to ask for Dennis, the manager.

I made my way across sawdust and mud in my Crocs and socks but couldn't find what looked like a manager's office. Another workman came walking toward me. I explained my interest. "Follow me," he said and led me to a door with no markings. He pushed the door open and I followed him to where two men were standing, talking. I introduced myself. "I'm staying at the Cassiar RV park and saw your mill and, to be honest, was like a kid who wanted to see how logs were made into lumber. I would understand if you don't think this a good idea. I don't have a hard hat and stuff."

The fellow immediately to my right, another man in a dirty fluorescent lime green vest, turned to the other fellow, a man about 45 years old dressed in white shirt and pants who kept tumbling a machine part in his right hand. The lime-green clad man asked the manager (who I later learned was the owner), "Want me to take him on a tour?" My new advocate hadn't shaved in about week and his grin was broken by missing front teeth, but he seemed enthusiastic about showing me the mill, which he later told me his father helped build in 1963. It's been operating ever since.

"Sure," the owner said. "Give him that hard hat," pointing to one hanging on the wall behind my new lime green vested friend who also reached for a small plastic bag and said as he handed me the hat, "And here are some earplugs. It gets pretty noisy out there."

Off we went. Over more sawdust and mud, up and down steps and planks of metal grates, ducking our heads to avoid overhead structures of steel. We would stop every so often and my guide would tell me what a piece of machinery was doing to cedar or hemlock as I would unplug one ear or the other depending on which side faced him at the moment. I loved it.

As we finished the tour I thanked him and said "I'm impressed that every man we saw had a job to do and was busy doing it. I didn't see any supervisor standing around, telling the men what to do."

"Well, that's 'cause I'm the supervisor," he said with a toothless smile. I shook his hand, thanked him again, and was happily on my way.

17 Give Yourself 90 Minutes

Give yourself 90 minutes to solve a problem with the RV before you call (and worse, pay) for help. It took us that long to solve the mystery of the slide that refused to retract. (Slides are sections of the coach that can be extended out from the body of the cab, enlarging the interior living space by about 18 inches, which makes a big difference.)

* * *

We awoke early one morning to make the border crossing back into the United States for the last time on the Alaska trip. We were told that these crossings can take more than an hour if you arrive there late in the morning. We finished our coffee and made our deposits in the camp's WC. Wilma had corralled the cat in her travel carrier. Parking brake on, engine on, I depressed the button on the RV console to retract the jacks. No problem. Jacks retracted.

The RV operator's manual advises you to retract the slide before you retract the jacks that level the coach. Why did I flip the sequence? We'd been on the road for more than 2 ½ months at that time in our trip but just violated the recommended steps for departure, which we had followed to the letter before. This is another point you'll better understand after you've driven an RV for a while. You make mistakes. No matter how many times you begin or end a leg of your journey, you will forget to do things you've always done before. You can put together a checklist, but you'll forget to use it.

That we retracted the jacks before the slide plays a role in this story, because the slide, which runs nearly the length of the driver's side of the coach, didn't retract when Wilma pushed the "IN" indicator of the rocker switch. (We would learn the name of this type of whatschamadoodle switch – a "rocker" -- in the process of trying to decipher the operator's manual instructions for retracting the slide.)

"Why'd we retract the jacks before the slide?" I asked Wilma, thinking that our mistake caused the slide to stall.

"I don't know," she replied.

"Ok, let's put the jacks down again and try the slide."

We did. The slide still didn't budge even after following the right sequence of steps.

"You know, we could have dislodged something last night when we put the car on the tow dolly, or maybe we put the coach out of balance when we did that," Wilma said.

"OK, let's take the car off the dolly and then try the slide."

We did. Slide still didn't slide.

We became desperate. Lines were surely forming that moment outside the border crossing. But we couldn't move an inch. Time to consult the Operator's Manual. You take this step only when all else fails because it is written by people who think everything is obvious, which it is to those who build or fix coaches and write these manuals. Social scientists label this phenomenon the "curse of knowledge." Experts forget the time they knew as little as a struggling couple with a slide stuck in the open position who can't get to the border crossing.

Consider the first steps the manual instructed us to follow in troubleshooting a slide that won't slide, which the manual called a "fault." The manual instructed us to check the "Fault Code LED" that was displayed beneath the rocker switch that controlled the extension of the slide. The manual provided a photo of the switch that looked nothing like ours but asked us to count the number of its red flashes. It then told us to check the Motor LED on a control box for its number of flashing green lights and then examine a chart that listed the number of red and green light flash combinations for a diagnosis of the problem and its possible solution. One such solution was to "Refer to TIP Sheet 82-S0533 for troubleshooting."

The manual also provided a photo of what we would find inside the panel but didn't tell us where to find the panel. Was it on the driver's or passenger's side? Front? Rear? I couldn't see any panel until I crawled between the steering wheel and driver's seat in desperation.

"Here's a panel. Please hand me a flashlight," I asked Wilma.

I opened the panel. It also looked NOTHING like the photo. There was no green, blinking LED light.

We spent the next 30 minutes looking for the mystery panel. We opened doors to fuses and circuit breakers, lifted one of the runners of the steps to see if the LED signal might be nestled among the coach batteries. It wasn't.

I began to think about knocking on other coach doors.

Has your slide ever not worked? I rehearsed to myself. Wilma at this same moment was saying "Maybe we should go to the office. They might know someone who knows how to fix this."

It was about 8:00 a.m. We had been working on the problem for an hour. We had some time to go before seeking other aid in our 90-minute rule.

We returned to the Manual, now nearing panic. Lines at the crossing must be two hours long by now, as drooping faces and shoulders belied these silent thoughts. But neither of us accused the other of being at fault about the fault. Neither of us raised our voice. We must have been exhausted from traveling so far for so long.

"Can the slide be moved manually?" we asked the Manual. Yes. The manual told us about "override modes," which allegedly permitted us to retract the slide and drive the RV somewhere for help. The manual listed nine steps and four notes about this procedure. I had to locate a vertical channel outside the coach and remove a screw from the "bulb seal" at the top of the channel.

We went outside. I couldn't locate the screw that was to be removed. I didn't even know what the vertical channel was. Nothing on our coach looked like the black and white photos in the manual. Wilma kept asking if we had the tool pictured in the manual to remove the bolts we couldn't find. We didn't. No matter. Wilma began to read more of the Manual aloud. It noted that, failing steps 1 through 9 (we didn't get past 1), it might be possible to retract the slide by accessing a "1/2-inch square drive tube." Right. Screw the manual. Let's think for a minute.

I remembered a little rocker switch next to the one that keeps the steps in open position when parked and the door is closed. I looked at the label on the switch. "Is 'coach' the same thing as' chassis'?" I asked.

'I don't know," Wilma replied.

I turned the rocker arm to "On," climbed back up the stairs to the driver's seat and turned on the motor. (This step is required for retracting both the jacks and the slide.) Engine running, I walked down the center of the coach to the rocker switch that controlled the slide and pressed the "In" side of the rocker. The slide slid.

After the slide had retracted fully, we retracted the jacks, strapped the car to its dolly, and edged out of the campground. About five minutes toward the border crossing, I turned to Wilma who was driving and asked, "Didn't we have the same problem with the slide back in March that we fixed by turning on the coach power?"

"Yeh, we did, didn't we?"

We made it to the border crossing, only two cars ahead

of us. We then followed Wilma's tactics for fast passage through customs.

How to speed through customs between the United States and Canada

We happened upon a foolproof way to speed through customs on our first crossing into Canada and would use it each time we drove back and forth across the border. The gist of the tactic was for Wilma to drive up to each crossing and give long answers to any border guard's questions. For example, a border guard at one of the crossings asked Wilma "How many days have you been in Canada?" Wilma would answer something like the following: "Well, we left [name of place] and stayed two nights at [name of next place], then we went on to [name of third and fourth destination]. I don't remember exactly, but I can get my calendar to tell you exact dates if you'd like." Or a guard might ask, "Any pets traveling with you?" to which Wilma would reply "Yes, our cat. She's in her travel carrier and has liked the trip so far. Would you like me to show you our cat's immunization papers? I can get them if you'd like."

Border agents (we encountered only men in this position) would begin rolling their eyeballs after two such exchanges. You could read the cartoon bubble above their heads as they said to themselves, "Oh, my God. This woman won't shut up. She wants to have a conversation with me. Get her out of here." Young men rarely want to engage in conversation with a woman their mother's age. Instead, they'd say, "Thank you, mam, you can be on your way." A smug grin painted our faces as we pulled away.

18 What You Learn from Travelling

One good thing about buying an RV is the incentive it creates to travel. "Why'd you buy the darn thing if you were just going to let it set in your driveway or storage lot?" And travel of any kind, via any means, is a good thing, in general. It reminds you of how little you know about so much. You can't help but ask questions you would have never thought to ask. Now granted, these questions and their answers aren't always earth-shattering. But you'll have a moment of self-satisfied ahahness. "Ahah! So that's why those bales of hay are bleach blond rather than green like freshly cut grass. They're not grass. They're bundled wheat!" "No wonder Crazy Horse never signed a peace treaty. He knew it wouldn't be kept." "So, General Philip Henry

Sheridan thought that killing buffalo was a more effective way of removing Native Americans from their lands than sending in the troops." I thought I was clever in concocting a theory that the word "Dakota" must have been a perverse pronunciation of the word "Lakota," which is what we heard and read about on the trip. No. A park ranger informed me that there are three dialects for the Lakota nation: Lakota, Dakota, and Nakota.

You also learn that tourists, like yourself, can be an easy mark for panhandlers. One of two Oglala Sioux women selling beadworks at the memorial for Wounded Knee warned us not to believe the three young men from their tribe who asked us for money to support a summer youth camp as we descended the steps of our coach in the memorial's parking lot. I had almost been reeled in by them when they opened a notebook that allegedly included artwork from these deserving children. The older of the two women selling her beadwork told us and other tourists that there was no such camp and that there was no museum of native art that the panhandlers had invited us to visit in a building across the highway from the memorial. Their cover blown, the young Lakota panhandlers skulked across the highway to their "museum."

The two Lakota women who busted the young panhandlers made their jewelry from local buffalo bone and teeth, horse hair, porcupine quill, and glass beads from China. They told us a story that their land had oil lying beneath it, but no one in their tribe wanted to drill for it because the profits would only be used to pay off the debts the tribe owed to the federal government. We later asked Matthew, a park ranger at a nearby station about this claim. He looked puzzled. "I've never heard of that," he said, "although I understand there are minerals further north that the tribe doesn't want to have mined for fear of what it would do to the land."

Wounded Knee

We went a little out of way to visit the Wounded Knee Memorial, site of a massacre of Sioux by U.S. troops in 1890. I had remembered the name, although not the details of what happened there so many years ago from reading Dee Brown's book, *Bury My Heart at Wounded Knee*. Brown, a librarian by profession, wrote a book about the "white man's" repeated betrayal of the "red man." Brown would become famous for her book, at least among the liberal college set of the 1970s.

I was surprised to find only a single sign to "commemorate" this event. The sign was red with white lettering on both sides. It was carefully written and painted, but still amateurish by the standards of national park service monuments, which it apparently is not. The sign now stands describing what took place at this site over 120 years ago. It took the sign makers about 300 words to describe the apparent missteps and misunderstanding of both white and red man, how Army troops in the confusion of battle turned guns on the Sioux encampment that included fellow soldiers trying to negotiate a peaceful end to the confrontation and to confiscate the arms that warriors had refused to give up. There were women and children and elderly in the camp as well, all of whom the Army had wanted to escort to a reservation but ended up gunning down from horseback as they fled their camp and the raging battle. A medicine man among the band of Native Americans had emboldened the warriors in camp to keep their guns and to use them against the more heavily armed U.S. troops because the Ghost Dance he had taught the warriors would render them impervious to the white man's bullets.

There now stands on this site, in addition to the sign, a parking lot and some wooden structures to house Native American craft-makers who sell their goods to curious white men and women. There is a graveyard atop the hill across the road as well as a community center that looks down on the grounds where the fighting took place. Many grave markers display the emblem of a branch of the military in which the deceased had served in WWII or the Korean or Vietnam wars. No other ethnic group in the United States volunteers for military service in greater proportion than Native Americans.

Fact checking may not be available

There is no word for "Sioux" among Sioux tribes, we were told by Matthew, the park service agent who is also an Oglala Sioux. "It's a French word," he told us, "that translates into 'snake in the grass.' It was a word stamped or imposed on the Seven Councils of the Lakota peoples by white men." It was used pejoratively, for the most part, as one would use a term to stigmatize another group as inferior to your own. Matthew, trying to soften these harsh sentiments, added that the word's less pejorative interpretation is of a long band of Lakota on horse and foot winding their way through the vast grasslands of the plains like a snake.

Fact checking Matthew's story weeks later might have earned him a Pinocchio by the <u>Washington Post</u>. There is some dispute as to the origin of the word "Sioux" according to authorities who have posted their knowledge online, but the one I found most persuasive asserted that the word was a truncation of the French spelling of a pejorative Ojibwa Indian word for little rattlesnake, Nadouessioux. I could find no definition that suggested: "snake in the grass."

But I did discover in this search for the etymology of "Sioux" that the Dakota Sioux used the term "Whiteman" pejoratively, likening him to a prankster.

But it was no ordinary Halloween variety prankster. It was one who engaged in incest, lust, theft, gluttony, and more. Take that Whiteman.

There was one story told to me by a Native American that was clearly told with "tongue in cheek." I asked a Sioux woman beading necklaces at Wounded Knee why I had seen three automobiles with cracked front windshields that morning like the car her son had driven away a few minutes before. She said in her Oglala Sioux English accent, "Yeh, I told him it used to be a nice car."

I pressed her on how it got to be not such a nice car. She cracked a smile and said, "He got mad at his girlfriend."

"He threw his girlfriend against the windshield?"

"No," she said, still smiling. "He was resmerized," emphasizing the word she or a friend had coined. I look puzzled, so she added, "You know, mesmerized on the reservation."

I smiled but must have looked like I still didn't understand. "Okay, he was probably drunk when he smashed his hand into the glass," she said. If she wasn't being truthful, she at least confirmed the narrative that must have painted my face.

19 Travel Tips

We learned a lot along the way to and from Alaska about RVing. Experience is an unforgiving instructor, but there's always a chance that one can learn from others' mistakes and encounters. Here are few I hope might ease your way down the road should you travel it in an RV.

Tip 1: How to stay in the middle of your lane

To drive a Class A RV in the middle of your lane, imagine a laser shooting from your left eye through the left side of your left knee. Continue to extend that beam outside the coach. It should fall on the broken white (or yellow) line that divides lanes. If it does, you're in the middle of your lane. This tip may vary depending on the style and size of your RV so come up with your own technique for protecting against the tendency, especially when beginning, to drive too far to the right of your lane.

Driving in the middle of your lane is a very useful skill and one that requires some practice. But it's useful in passing cars and trucks with some confidence or in negotiating lanes that are redirected to accommodate road repair crews ahead. Driving in the middle of your lane is one of only three things you must do while driving an RV. The other two are being able to stop before crushing the car in front of you and observing the speed limit.

Tip 2: Pack a ladder

Take along a lightweight ladder and window washing materials to clean the windshield after a summer's day travel. Or buy a brush with an extended handle. If your RV has a large semi-flat front windshield like ours, a wide assortment of bugs will smash into it in mindless sacrifice. They'll be as sticky as they are numerous. Windshield wipers and cleaning fluid will simply smear their dead bodies in flowing arcs across the window. (I swear that bugs in Canada take the shape of a maple leaf when they smash into your windshield.)

Tip 3: Don't panic if you forget to pack something

You can order that item on Amazon and have it delivered to a campground you'll soon visit. Wilma texted one such campground where we were to stay in about a week and asked if they'd hold a package for us if delivered before we arrived. They did (although not all campgrounds will). We were practiced in this tactic, having used it once before because I forgot my passport at home. I think we were driving through Indiana when Wilma turned to me and asked, "Did you remember to pack your passport?" After an expletive, I confessed "No." Our neighbors, Bill and Bernice, were nice enough to fetch my passport from my underwear drawer in our bedroom and mail it to a campground where it awaited us about a week later.

Tip 4: Don't poop in your own nest

Don't poop in your own RV if you can avoid it. And avoiding it is easy if you stop at RV campgrounds with public restrooms. Getting rid of pee is troubling enough. Why mess with solid waste too? You can also stop to relieve yourself at thousands of stores, restaurants, and welcome centers. They've got real plumbing, not those flexible three-inch "pipes" that you attach to the underbelly of your rig that run another 10 feet or so to a hole in the ground at your campsite.

Tip 5: How fast to drive

Your RV has a "sweet spot." Ours is at about 65 mph on a level highway, the engine is running at about 2,000 rpms. It talks to you. "This speed is just right. I feel good. I could run like this all day." The RV is a long-distance runner in the middle of a 15,000-meter race. Long, loping strides bounce off the track, effortlessly. Breathing is measured, easy. No need to make a move, you've got plenty of time, especially with 80 gallons of gas in your belly.

Tip 6: Stay in the right lane

Stay in the right lane of a multi-lane highway (unless you can't). There are several reasons for this. First, if a semi or gust of wind blows your rig to the right, you'll hit the rumble strip, not another vehicle as you might, for example, if running in the middle lane of three. Second, you won't have cars passing you on your right, where you are likely to have a blind spot. Third, it's been my experience that the right lane moves faster than others in heavy traffic.

Tip 7: Beware of exploding pee

Our coach holds its accessible plumbing in a separate compartment in the "basement." Your hose for fresh water and your flexible tube for waste discharge fit through a hole in the bottom of this compartment. The waste discharge outlet, which has a cover cap, will look you straight in the eye when you kneel to connect the plumbing to external sources on a Class A like ours. We purchased a "see through" 90-degree elbow to attach to this outlet so that our waste tube could be fed directly into this elbow from the opening in the base of the compartment. A good purchase.

You'll put the cap on this elbow while traveling from site to site. And although your waste valves are "closed" during your trip, I always found about an inch or so of liquid waiting for me when I connected the discharge pipe at the new site.

Gas forms in the see-through 90-degree elbow as you shake, rattle, and roll down the highway in scalding summer temperatures in places like South Dakota, California, and Arizona. That inch of wastewater can explode in your face if you open the cap too quickly. Trust me. I speak from experience. Exploding pee in your face is not pleasant. Release the gas slowly, using heavy plastic gloves to muffle escaping liquid and gas as you unscrew the cap.

Tip 8: Deal with anger

You will get into an argument with your spouse, partner, or significant other if he or she is involved in helping drive the coach, hitch the tow dolly, back up the RV, or whatever. Should your anger rise to a boil, my advice is to let it out and put it behind you. You've got to spend a lot of time with that person in tight quarters in the RV, and perhaps the rest of your life outside of it, so it's best to get over your anger.

This general rule can be applied to the reprobates who speed past you and turn abruptly in front of you. It's okay to swear or yell at them within the confines of your coach, but I recommend against using the horn, which is a formidable instrument on an RV. And don't flip them the bird. You're unlikely to remember the carry laws in the state through which you happen to be passing at that moment.

Tip 9: Disguising outside noise

If you enjoy sleeping with the windows of your coach open or dislike being refrigerated constantly by AC during the summer but are distracted by the nearby noise of cars and trains, turn on the fan over your bed (assuming you have one and the weather is dry and warm). This may also work with other fans on the coach or bring a fan and run it during the night. Not only does it circulate the fresh air that it helps draw into the coach, it creates a white noise that can block out external sounds, except for the refreshing songs of morning birds.

Tip 10: On bathhouses and toilets

Many campgrounds install keypads on the entry doors to showers and toilets. Make sure you remember their code as you step lightly across grass and gravel to answer Mother Nature's call. Do not tempt her by failing to record that number in your memory or on a piece of paper in your pocket.

Tip 11: Debating while traveling

I wonder if there's a name for a tactic that my wife would often use in debates or arguments we would have while driving. She'd clearly be losing the argument (at least in my mind) when she'd say something that was undisputedly true but had nothing to do with the argument. It threw me off for a while, sometimes for quite a while. You might think about using this technique yourself.

Tip 12: Trailing another car or truck

Find a semi, car, or van going the speed at which you feel comfortable traveling and follow it using a four-second (rather than two-second) rule for safe braking distances.

Tip 13: Buy a GPS

Buy a GPS and move it to the passenger side dash. This makes the passenger a navigator and removes a distraction from the driver. It also lets you know as a passenger how fast your wife is driving. (Not all GPSs report your speed. You might want to look for one that does.)

Tip 14: Look out for dips

Use the lines in the road, especially the white shoulder line, to spot upcoming dips and mounds in the road. Take them seriously. You can go airborne, ripping off front and rear bumpers on landing. We heard of two coaches whose airbags exploded after driving across these dips too quickly in the Yukon.

Tip 15: Dealing with broken windshields

If your windshield is hit by a flying rock, ask the manager of your next campground to recommend someone who repairs these cracks before they begin to spread across your windshield. Such a person typically comes to your site and drills small holes at the end of the spider legs of cracks and then fills these holes with an epoxy that is intended to stop the crack's continual creep. Spare windows are not readily available and must be ordered a couple weeks in advance. Shipping alone to a remote location can cost hundreds of dollars.

Tip 16: Look down the road

You can stop the back-and-forth wobble of your coach by looking about 100 to 150 yards down the road. Your corrections will be less pronounced when responding to sudden burst of wind as you look to move to the center of your lane that far away.

Tip 17: More about waste and plumbing

You may be able to minimize this residual wastewater (see a previous tip) by flushing your toilet a couple of times after this wastewater appears to have been discharged. There are parts of the wastewater tank that do not fully vacate when you open the valve.

Interestingly (if you're into plumbing – which cannot be avoided as an owner), your RV has two kinds of waste, which some brilliant engineer, manufacturer, or marketing expert labeled "black waste water" and "grey waste water." These are not accurate descriptions for the liquids and semi-solid waste that flow from each of these pipes. Had I been consulted, I would have named "black" as "P water" to indicate "pee, poop, and papier de toilette." That's what is intended to flow through the coach's intestinal tract when you pull the handle so labeled. Or I would have labeled it "T water" for a simpler descriptive initial for "toilet." Similarly, I would have called "grey" the "S wastewater" for soapy or sink water. Think source or content rather than color.

Tip 18: The "hip tip"

Make 90 degree turns when your hip has moved to the point on the adjacent road to which you want the coach to end up after a hard turn.

Tip 19: It's metric in Canada

Canada measures itself in meters, kilometers, and liters, not considering the trouble this poses its poor southern neighbors. If your coach is like ours, you won't be able to read the tiny red numbers on the speedometer for km/hr (kilometers per hour) and will have to translate Maximum 50 km/hr on a Canadian road sign into miles/hour if you care about obeying the speed limit. Here's a little tip for doing so. Multiply the first digit of a two-digit Canadian road sign by six to arrive at an approximate translation from kilometers into miles per hour. That is to say, 50 km/hr is 5 x 6 = 30 miles/hour.

20 Lasting Impressions

Travel enriches the mind and senses. How better to feel the speed of the Yukon River's current carrying prospectors toward the fulfillment of their dreams of wealth in the Klondike than to stand on its banks? Why would you come to question how and why 60 million buffalo were slaughtered on America's plains unless you saw the vast openness of the plains and can imagine hundreds of thousands of these animals grazing alongside the highways you drive across in South Dakota? How could you better feel the injustice of the United States government forcing Native Americans to march from their native lands in Georgia to desolate reservations in Oklahoma, many of them dying on their way, unless you saw the marker that commemorated that "Trail of Tears" and saw in your mind's eye those families crossing the path that now stands before you?

But am I a deeper-thinking person having learned facts or asked questions I hadn't previously asked? Did I learn something about myself (beyond being reminded of the limits of my knowledge)? What's the point of all this travel? I think the simple answer is that travel helps me better appreciate the variety of our existence and the constancy of human folly. Perhaps that is enough.

* * *

The color of streams fed by melting snows varies with its source. The streams fed by glaciers near the Ice Field Visitors' Center in Canada were milky brown, carrying particles of dirt being blown into and excavated by the streams of melting glacial ice. These waters downstream were still milky but green like a glass of heavy creme to which you've added drops of green food coloring and stirred. Many of the snow-fed streams and lakes we saw throughout Canada were as turquoise as Native American jewelry you'd buy in Santa Fe.

* * *

Sure, the Canadian Rockies are majestic, purplishy so. They're gigantic, a single mountain taking up enough space on a map to squash the entire city of St. Louis.

Some have sharp serrated edges. Others are languid, round, like a naked 600-pound woman lying on her back, immobile, asleep.

Mountains morph into monsters and animals. I saw one that looked like Hans Solo's partner, Chewbacca, and another that looked like the grey, dusty back of an elderly elephant. But even the elephant whispered to anyone willing to patiently listen (or willing to pop a peyote button). The elephant mountain spoke of wisdom, not in words but as a quality it possessed, a virtue it represented, an attribute one should strive to attain. No matter how you describe the physical characteristics of these landscapes, they move you spiritually. The mountains, valleys, wide streams, river beds, and glaciers lead you to think that God must have created such a land. It's easy to understand how a member of the First Nation would have thought that powerful spirits, both good and evil, forged these mountains and cut rivers through them.

* * *

We traveled through forests along the Cassiar highway in Canada that had been struck by fire. The fires weren't the 200 or so recent ones that we outdistanced in British Columbia, or the 40 or so that had choked us in the Yukon and Oregon, but ones that had raged a few years before we happened upon them. The landscapes left by these wildfires were like black pen and ink drawings. The trees, I was surprised to see, hadn't burned to the ground. Their tall trunks remained upright, denuded of leaves, but still holding outstretched arms. Their barks had remained charred black, at least those trees that wind and rain had not denuded. The trees whose blackened bark had fallen to the ground stood like dry, grey bones.

*   *   *

We traveled across Oregon and saw little of it. Two large wildfires whitewashed the landscape with smoke that spread across much of the western part of the state and into Northern California. We passed up the campground we had booked in southern Oregon to outpace the smoke and did so only after driving south into California for more than an hour, the smoke subsiding as we reached Mt. Shasta. But one good thing: we evacuated our house in Florida three months in advance of Hurricane Irma.

*   *   *

We're too cheap to buy a satellite dish for the RV. Besides, I read somewhere that satellite reception is bad in Alaska, which we found to be true. Too many trees and mountains in the way of the satellite's signal to a dish that – given the Northern latitude -- must be pointed at the horizon to snag an image.

There are RV campgrounds that provide "cable" TV hookups. Your menu of stations often consists (at least in the northern reaches of North America) of two to eight analog channels. News channels are usually not on the menu; but when they are, it's a local channel, Fox News, or CNN. Wilma once expressed regret at one campground manager that they didn't offer MSNBC. He asked what MSNBC was. "It's like a left-wing version of Fox News," she responded.

"No, we don't have anything like that, although there's a news channel that's kind of middle of the road that my wife likes." He pointed to the channel on a long list that he had handed Wilma. "I'm a Second Amendment guy myself. If I don't like what you got to say, I got the right to shoot you." Wilma thanked him and headed for safety.

There are a couple of plausible explanations for the choice of Fox News among so many RV campgrounds in the rural western parts of the United States and Canada. First, the network may be a bargain in the woods. Second, it may be the channel of choice among a plurality or majority of RV owners who visit and/or stay in these areas. I don't know whether either of these possibilities is true. I turned the channel from Fox News to MSNBC in the lodge of the campground in Red Bluff, California when no one else was in the building, only to find it back at Fox the next time I looked. My guess is that there simply aren't enough liberal Californians who own RVs and travel the country to shift the balance of demand toward more left-wing-nut-job channels.

* * *

I didn't appreciate the vastness of the West prior to our journey. You can hear or read about it, but there's no better way to understand what that means than to drive through it. You come to feel that vastness in your bones. You can smell it and feel it on your skin. It's a tactile understanding that your body understands; not just your brain.

* * *

It's not the billboard I saw on the road that depicted a newborn baby and read "Proof There Is a God" that sways me toward such a belief. It's the pungent smell of a farm: its dirt, manure, livestock, cut grass, and hay. It's as if I can smell the creation of life in the cool, moist morning air. Maybe I think this about farms because there is no place more vulnerable to the whims of Mother Nature or God than farms that prosper or fail on matters beyond the control of those who work its soil through long and hard labor. Or maybe it's because those smells remind me of my family's vacations in Texas when I was a boy, largely innocent of the world's evil.

* * *

One evening while camping near Valemount, British Columbia I saw a sunset that looked like one you would see in a polluted urban sky. I pointed this out to Wilma, who agreed. Strange, we both thought. Wilma was skimming Facebook at the time when she read a message from a friend who lives in California and whose son lives in British Columbia. She told Wilma that forest fires were blazing in a mountain valley to our southeast. Roads were being closed, people evacuated from their homes, and travelers rerouted. We were lucky. The wildfires would trail us by a day as we made our way north and west. I couldn't help but wonder how First Nations' people, whose land this once was, would have known how far away wildfires raged and whether their village or camp would be in danger at morning's rise.

*   *   *

Wilma met a first generation Black Foot who was cleaning the laundry room at the campsite near Shelby, Montana. He told her that he left the reservation to escape the fate of half his high school friends who had become addicted to drugs and alcohol by age 18. He had made it to 30 years old and was proud to tell Wilma that he and his wife supported four children.

"If alcohol and drugs don't get you, gambling is an addiction that will ruin your life," he told Wilma. I guess casinos made some Native Americans rich and enslaved others, perhaps far greater in number than those who prosper from them. It's not difficult to imagine the numbers affected by a gambling addiction insofar as casinos are everywhere in Montana. Gas stations, for example, set aside small, windowless rooms inside where you can find a dozen slot machines. Ditto for motels, all in addition to the large casinos that spring up in remote areas linked to the world by interstate highways.

* * *

States have personalities. It might be better to say that different states market themselves differently. I'm using that term in the broadest sense of everything an organization – or, in this case, a state – does and says that is seen and heard by the public. You can see it in the types of billboards that line their highways, their speed limits, terrain, and more.

Billboards offer a peek into the values of the communities through which you travel. I'm always struck while driving through the South of the juxtaposition of billboards about sex shops (e.g., Adult Central SuperStore, Lion's Den Super Store) and religion (e.g., "Are you going to heaven or hell? Call 555 555-5555 to find out," "The only way to heaven is through the blood of Christ"), or the messages from Jesus (e.g., "I'm still in control – Jesus," "Have you made a decision? – Jesus"). I wonder if Jesus is asking if you've made a decision about visiting the Lion's Den. I don't know if there's a battle being waged for your body and soul in such states as Georgia or whether those sex stores are a sign of the moral decay of Georgians who prey on Sunday and visit sex shops Monday through Saturday. We passed another billboards in North Carolina that read "Where are you going? Heaven or Hell?" We were actually on our way to Florida.

The maximum speed limit jumps from 70 to 80 when you cross from Minnesota to South Dakota where the exit ramps post no speed limits and the billboards tell you it's okay again to buy fireworks, having suffered through its prohibition in Minnesota. The grass and crops thirsted for water as we entered in South Dakota, while the crops in Minnesota had their thirst quenched. I wonder how mother nature knows where the state borders are.

South Dakota has no toll roads (at least along the path we drove), but plenty of five-foot-tall bundles of rolled hay, firework stores at every highway exit, and billboard ads for universities. A sign posted over the hand dryer in the men's bathroom of a campground near Mitchell, South Dakota read, "I'd rather have a gun in my hand than a cop on the phone." The sign had faux bullet holes below this saying and, below it, the caption "Second Amendment."

The sense you get of the state is that it's raw, less sophisticated than, say, Minnesota where you find green fields of corn and soybeans that are peppered with fields of wind turbines. Indiana boasts of RV dealerships and fireworks. It feels like dirt behind the ears. Wisconsin adds the Packers and cheese to the RV/fireworks staple.

* * *

Wilma and I just finished touring the Soulard neighborhood of St. Louis and were heading to my high school 50th reunion dinner in South County in our Prius. I had the GPS on, but took a wrong turn and hesitated as I tried to figure out how to get back on the right path. A black man in his late 30s pulled up beside our car and rolled down his window. I asked Wilma to roll down her passenger-side window so we could hear what he was saying to us, although I feared the worst. St. Louis had been the "Murder Capital of the United States" for two years running and one of its suburbs, Ferguson, was the site of not too distant racial tensions surrounding the shooting of a young black man, Michael Brown, by a police officer who was acquitted of any wrongdoing.

"Hey, I saw your license plate. I used to live in Osceola County too," he said. "Where you going?"

I said I was trying to get on I-55 going south. He said, "Follow me. I'll take you there."

My wife and I were stunned. Neither of us had ever had anyone offer that kind of help. We followed him for about five minutes as he made turns that our GPS disavowed, but I wasn't going to disrespect the work of a good Samaritan helping two old people from Florida who didn't know their way. Screw the GPS. We saw the sign that instructed us to turn right at the next intersection to South I-55. I pulled alongside the Samaritan's car, honked, and waved thanks.

* * *

If you've got a 30-foot rig, towing a car with a hitch adds another 17 feet to the rear. That requires you to worry about entering a street or driveway whose path cannot be seen. You may not be able to turn around, and you can't back up with a car in tow. Your tow dolly will likely jackknife if you back up more than a few feet.

* * *

The centers of small towns across the United States have become "Historic Districts." This designation may mean that you'll find an antique shop or two, a restaurant selling fried, bar food with margarita specials on Friday night, and a co-op art gallery staffed by volunteer, retired school teachers who always wanted to paint and now have three portraits of their Shih Tzu hanging on the gallery wall, priced never to sell at $125 each. There are still plenty of boarded-up stores that once housed bustling bakeries, furniture stores, and Five-and-Dimes.

The state may have granted a small town like Millville, New Jersey a few million dollars to convert the remaining movie house into a performing arts center that draws people from the diaspora beyond the town a few times a year to hear tribute bands from the 1950s sing the same songs they have for more than 50 years. The towns are fighting a tough battle, but I worry that it's futile for many of them. Chain stores located near the exit ramps of four-lane highways that now bypass these towns are large, ruthless, efficient, profit-seeking international corporations. Their logistical efficiencies and purchasing power play the grim reaper for the small stores in many of these towns. And Internet shopping has added nail in their coffins.

Some small towns have avoided this fate, and many of these share common characteristics, the most telling of which is the location of the county seat, natural or man made attractions that create tourist destination, or a local college or university. Charming Geneva, New York hosts Hobart and Smith College; vibrant Ithaca NY is blessed with Cornell University and Ithaca College; historic Claremont, California enjoys Claremont, Harvey Mudd, and Pomona Colleges; idyllic Blacksburg, Virginia entertains Virginia Tech; Oxford, Mississippi embraces the University of Mississippi; picturesque Laramie, Wyoming boasts the

University of Wyoming. And New York City embraces Barnard College (just seeing if you're paying attention). The students who attend these colleges and universities pump millions of dollars into these small local economies with parents' hard-earned income from all over the globe.

Similar processes are afoot in city neighborhoods like the one in which I grew up in St. Louis. I could -- as a 10-year-old kid – walk to a bakery, grocery store, cleaners, drug store, bicycle shop, barber, ice cream shop, grade school, church, movie theater, a park with a public swimming pool, playgrounds and picnic areas, baseball fields, restaurants, and taverns (to find my dad if I needed him). Most of these stores no longer exist.

* * *

Your comfort level with your RV changes with each trip, each mile driven. It moved for me from the fear of being blown off the highway by a crosswind or a passing 18-wheeler to looking forward to driving to my step-daughter's house and "camping" in her driveway to babysit her family's four kids. It took me about 10,000 miles of driving to achieve that level of zen.

You can see the comfort level rise in the speeds at which we drove (probably five mph faster than when we started out), our willingness to pass slower vehicles, and the ease with which we make left and right turns on city streets. This is not the say we have become totally relaxed. You must remain vigilant while driving an RV, alert to the street signs that might leap out at you and decapitate a rear-view mirror. You must be alert to lowlife drivers who MUST pass you on the right as a highway entrance ramp nears its end.

There's a lesson here for those who want to experience what driving an RV is about by renting one and driving about 1,000 miles on a week's trip. You won't become comfortable with the RV unless you've already driven trucks for a living or graduated from pop-ups to fifth wheels, to Class C before wrestling with a Class A coach. How will you learn in a week all the lessons we discovered on our voyage unless, of course, you study this book from front to end?

We must confess that despite cracked windshield, stuck steps, leaking coolant, faulty refrigerator, pee exploding in my face, and an open and immovable slide, we didn't experience all that could have gone wrong. Those are the stories you hear as a "First Timer." We didn't, for example, lose our awning to a late afternoon gust of wind, which we witnessed in a Canadian campground. We didn't have a tire blow out while traveling 65 miles an hour. We didn't tear off our front or back bumper of the RV.

* * *

I was, toward the end of our journey, beginning to feel like an astronaut who had been weightless for weeks as he orbited the Earth and had to be hospitalized upon his return because his bones had lost density and his muscles, mass. That's how I felt when I landed at home in Florida after 3 ½ months on the road with a few more pounds to carry around Disney World.

* * *

Much of our journey followed or crossed famous trails. We retraced parts of Lewis and Clark's expedition of 1804-1805 along the Missouri River in South Dakota. We drove the AlCan highway that followed an aerial trail of 18,000 planes that skipped along airfields from British Columbia through Alaska on their way to the Soviet Union to aid in the war against Germany and Japan as part of the Lend/Lease program of WWII. We detoured to Skagway, Alaska to walk the streets where prospectors lost their stakes to the likes of scoundrel Soapy Smith and his gang or lugged a ton of supplies up the White Pass trail on their way to hunt for gold in the Klondike in 1898. We drove to Fairbanks along the same path that prospectors traveled by less comfortable means on their way to the next gold rush in 1902. We crossed the Chisholm Trail in Oklahoma, which cattlemen used to drive herds from ranches in Texas to railheads in Kansas after the Civil War, and parts of the Trail of Tears in Georgia along which over 4,000 Native Americans from tribes in the Southeast United States lost their lives in forced marches. And our final trail was one many people each year make on their way to the Magic Kingdom to visit princesses and pirates.

21 The End, For Now

An older colleague with whom I worked at Carnegie
Mellon University years ago was frequently asked by
people who first met him whether he had worked all his
life. "Not yet," would always be his reply. My wife
and I have just finished a year driving an RV. We're
not quite done yet.

Since our return from our Alaska trip, we've had the
front windshield replaced, although we disputed the
"expedited" delivery charges, which were ultimately
resolved in our favor. We took the RV to an authorized
Winnebago dealer to solve the mystery of leaking
radiator fluid, which they didn't. But a Ford dealership
did when they found and mended a pinhole in a flexible
line from the radiator along the underbelly of the coach

to the hot water heater. We spent Thanksgiving back in Arlington, Virginia, parked in a driveway with our long extension cord supplying the coach with sufficient juice from an outdoor outlet, and enjoyed turkey dinner and more with kids and grandkids. And we visited with old friends in Fernandina Beach, Florida, while we camped in a beautiful Florida State campground at Fort Clinch State Park on Amelia Island.

There are a few obvious advantages to traveling via RV when compared to other forms of transportation. You can sleep in your own bed, pee in your own pot, shower in your own shower, cook in your own kitchen, and lounge in your own "living room." A couple of these advantages can save you money, although that's more than offset by the cost of gas at 8-10 miles per gallon that you guzzle on the road. And some of the "conveniences" are offset by the fact that you're required to become a sanitation engineer, putting on thick gloves, dumping waste into a hole in the ground, cleaning and reusing the flexible tubing through which waste escapes, disconnecting the waste hose, shutting down the hot water heater, turning off the propane that fuels the stove and heater, and on.

Whether an RV makes sense for you ultimately depends on what you value. Do you prefer to see the world or that part of it that you can only drive to? Do you want to take your pets with you on your journeys or do you feel comfortable leaving them with friends or other animal caregivers? Do you prefer to prepare your own meals or eat someone else's processed food? Do you prefer to sleep in your own bed or risk being bitten by bed bugs? (Okay, that question might be a little slanted.) Would you rather lay underneath a tow dolly to secure your car to it or get to the airport two hours in advance of your flight? Do you prefer to manage your own plumbing or not think about what happens when you flush?

We're now planning our second major trip, this time to the Maritime Provinces of Canada. I guess we must be at least a little nuts.

NOTES

4   **A class C is built:** On the differences between
        different classes of RV, see https://rv-
        roadtrips.thefuntimesguide.com/rv_class/.

11   **We tend not to join groups**: A paraphrase of
        Groucho Marx's reported quip in resigning from the
        Friars' Club, "I don't want to belong to any club that
        would accept me as one of its members." "In
        Hollywood" by Erskine Johnson, Dunkirk Evening
        Observer, October 20, 1949, page 22, Column 5,
        Dunkirk, New York. (NewspaperArchive)

21   **I divined the five percent rule**: I've always been
        impressed with Vilfredo Pareto's 80:20 rule. Pareto
        was an Italian economist, writing in the early 1900s,
        who observed that 80 percent of the income in Italy
        was earned by 20 percent of the population and that
        this ratio applied to many phenomena. It's used
        frequently in describing a general principal in
        fundraising among universities and other non-profit
        institutions: 80 percent of your donations will come
        from 20 percent of your donors. See, for example,
        Wylie, Peter B. *Baseball, Fundraising, and the
        80/20 Rule.* Hartford, CN: Case, Lockwood,
        Brainard. 2008. In business management, 80
        percent of your results allegedly come from 20
        percent of your efforts, according to Koch, Richard.
        The 80/20 Principle: The Secret of Achieving More

with Less. New York: Doubleday, 1998.

22   **...five percent of people who voted for Hillary Clinton**: The results of a survey conducted by PPP and reported on the Rachel Maddow Show, MSNBC, January 25, 2017. For more complete results, see http://www.publicpolicypolling.com/.../PPP_Releas e_National_1... as accessed January 28, 2018.

22   **... about five percent of infants**: Kagan, Jerome. *The Temperamental Thread*. NY: Dana Foundation, 2010.

22   **Second, five percent of the adult American population**: http://www.journalism.org/2013/10/11/how-americans-get-tv-news-at-home/ as accessed 10/25/17

22   **And third, about five percent of Americans believe**: Hochschild, Jennifer L. and Katherine Levine Einstein. *Do Facts Matter?* Norman, OK: University of Oklahoma Press, 2015, page 8.

36   **I guess it's the inactive ingredients**: Swanson, Ana. "Big Pharmaceutical Companies are Spending Far More on Marketing than Research." *Washington Post*. February 11, 2015. https://www.washingtonpost.com/news/wonk/wp/20 15/02/11/big-pharmaceutical-companies-are-spending-far-more-on-marketing-than-

research/?utm_term=.cb82cfc334b9 as accessed
January 5, 2018.

55   **Social scientists label this phenomenon**: Camerer,
      C.F., G. Loewenstein, and M. Weber. "The Curse of
      Knowledge in Economic Settings: An Experimental
      Analysis." *Journal of Political Economy* 97 (1989):
      1232-54. See also Hinds, Pamela J. "The Curse of
      Expertise: The Effects of Expertise and Debiasing
      Methods on Predicting Novice Performance."
      Journal of Experimental Psychology: Applied 9
      (1999): 205-21. A very entertaining and insightful
      discussion of this phenomenon can be found in
      Heath, Chip and Dan Heath. *Made to Stick: Why
      Some Ideas Survive and Others Die.* New York:
      Random House, 2007.

55   **Consider the first steps the manual**: Operator's
      Manual Supplement. 2017 Vista. Winnebago
      Company. Section on Power Gear DigiSync Slideout
      System, pages 2-4.

62   **the one I found most persuasive**: see
      http://spot.colorado.edu/~koontz/faq/etymology.htm.

76   **The centers of small towns**: McFarqhar, Larissa.
      "Where the Small-Town American Dream Lives
      On." *The New Yorker.* November 13, 2017.
      https://www.newyorker.com/magazine/2017/11/13/
      where-the-small-town-american-dream-lives-on as
      accessed December 31, 2017. For a graphical
      display of the dramatic and comparative changes
      taking place in small town America, see Calderon,

Angela. "The Divide Between America's Prosperous Cities and Struggling Small Towns – In 20 Charts." *Wall Street Journal*. December 29, 2017 https://www.wsj.com/articles/the-divide-between-americas-prosperous-cities-and-struggling-small-townsin-20-charts-1514543401 as accessed December 30, 2017.

ABOUT THE AUTHOR

Robert W. Pearson ushered at the first of his brother's three weddings at age 11 and warmed the bench on a basketball team playing in the Salvation Army league while in high school in St. Louis, Missouri. Beyond these early accomplishments, he later earned a PhD in political science from the University of Chicago, after which he worked to promote research in the social sciences and improvements in the nation's statistical system. Really. His last job before retiring several years ago was to teach in the public administration program at the University of Pennsylvania where he authored a shoulda-been-better-selling textbook in applied statistics, *Statistical Persuasion.*

Printed in Great Britain
by Amazon

32541215R00078